PHP Basic Recipe

Creating a User Registration Membership System

Third Edition

Onaje Johnston

PHP Basic Recipe

Creating a User Registration Membership System, Third Edition

Copyright © 2014 Onaje Johnston

First published: January 2011

Table of Contents

Preface

What is in This Version

The PHP developers have deprecated the original MySQL database extension. Eventually the mysql_* functions provided by this extension will be removed from PHP. The developers are recommending that PHP coders should instead use PHP Data Objects (PDO) or the improved, MySQLi extension. PDO is a database connection abstraction layer providing a uniform method of accessing multiple databases. This book covers using the MySQLi extension which includes support for features that are available in newer versions of the MySQL database server.

Suggested Use:

This book was written to help a beginner to intermediate level PHP programmer become more familiar with creating a database driven application. This is not a 'production' ready application. I do not recommend that you run the code without making it more secure. **I do not supply secure code**. There is no design provided; you must add the HTML/CSS for the design into the code. Use this application as the basis for your own. Add security, design and further customize to suit your specific needs.

Suggested Minimum Level of Experience: Advanced Beginner/Intermediate

You must be familiar with creating and debugging scripts using PHP and or MySQL before attempting to code this application. I make no attempt to explain every single line of code. I assume you are familiar with the basic syntax of PHP, variables, functions, conditional structures etc. and how to create tables, insert, delete, and update records via SQL (Structured Query Language) in a MySQL database server via PHP.

I also assume that you know to consult the PHP or MySQL manuals if you see a PHP function, SQL command or error message that you are not familiar with; or use a search engine to locate further reference material. You can access your MySQL database and make changes to tables, via the shell or a GUI (Graphical User Interface) program, e.g. PHPMyAdmin.

Code Download

A zipped archive of the code can be downloaded from http://phpbasicrecipe.com

1. Converting from the old PHP MySQL extension to the MySQLi extension

Many PHP programmers have not updated their code to use the MySQLi extension or the PDO extension. There is a MySQLi Converter Tool available which can convert a single file or a whole folder. This tool, or one like it, might be the answer to your conversion needs. But if you would prefer to do the conversion yourself as a learning exercise or do not like the code produced by the conversion tool, continue reading.

Converting or updating your code from MySQL to MySQLi is not a one-to-one equivalency. There are functions in MySQL that are not present in MySQLi. Though some function names are similar, there are differences in how the functions operate. The chart below lists some database functions used to create the registration application.

PHP MySQL to MySQLi Equivalency Function Chart

MySQL Function	Description	MySQLi OOP Version MySQLi Procedural Version	Description
mysql_affected_rows()	Get number of affected rows in previous MySQL operation	mysqli::affected_rows mysqli_affected_rows()	Gets the number of affected rows in a previous MySQL operation
mysql_close()	Close MySQL connection	mysqli::close mysqli_close()	Closes a previously opened database connection
mysql_connect()	Open a connection to a MySQL Server	mysqli::__construct mysqli_connect()	Open a new connection to the MySQL server

MySQL Function	Description	MySQLi OOP Version MySQLi Procedural Version	Description
mysql_data_seek()	Move internal result pointer	mysqli_result::data_seek() mysqli_data_seek()	Adjusts the result pointer to an arbitrary row in the result
mysql_errno()	Returns the numerical value of the error message from previous MySQL operation	mysqli::errno mysqli_errno()	Returns the error code for the most recent function call
mysql_error()	Returns the text of the error message from previous MySQL operation	mysqli::error mysqli_error()	Returns a string description of the last error
mysql_fetch_array()	Fetch a result row as an associative array, a numeric array, or both	mysqli_result::fetch_all() mysqli_fetch_all() mysqli_result::fetch_array() mysqli_fetch_array()	Fetches all result rows and returns the result set as an associative array, a numeric array, or both. Available only with mysqlnd. Fetch a result row as an associative, a numeric array, or both
mysql_fetch_assoc()	Fetch a result row as an associative array	mysqli_result::fetch_assoc() mysqli_fetch_assoc()	Fetch a result row as an associative array
mysql_fetch_field()	Get column information from a result and return as an object	mysqli_result::fetch_field() mysqli_fetch_field()	Returns the next field in the result set

Chapter 1: Converting from the old PHP MySQL extension to the MySQLi extension

MySQL Function	Description	MySQLi OOP Version MySQLi Procedural Version	Description
mysql_fetch_object()	Fetch a result row as an object	mysqli_result::fetch_object() mysqli_fetch_object()	Returns the current row of a result set as an object
mysql_fetch_row()	Get a result row as an enumerated array	mysqli_result::fetch_row() mysqli_fetch_row()	Get a result row as an enumerated array
mysql_free_result()	Free result memory	mysqli_result::free(), mysqli_result::close, mysqli_result::free_result mysqli_free_result()	Frees the memory associated with a result
mysql_insert_id()	Get the ID generated in the last query	mysqli::insert_id mysqli_insert_id()	Returns the auto generated id used in the last query
mysql_num_fields()	Get number of fields in result	mysqli_result::field_count mysqli_num_fields()	Get the number of fields in a result
mysql_num_rows()	Get number of rows in result	$mysqli_result::num_rows mysqli_num_rows()	Gets the number of rows in a result
mysql_query()	Send a MySQL query	mysqli::query() mysqli_query()	Performs a query on the database
mysql_real_escape_string()	Escapes special characters in a string for use in an SQL statement	mysqli::real_escape_string() mysqli_real_escape_string()	Escapes special characters in a string for use in an SQL statement, taking into account the current charset of the connection

MySQL Function	Description	MySQLi OOP Version MySQLi Procedural Version	Description
mysql_result()	Get result data	*There is no equivalent to mysql_result function, try one of the following instead: mysqli_result::fetch_all() mysqli_fetch_all()	Fetches all result rows and returns the result set as an associative array, a numeric array, or both. * Available only with mysqlnd.
		mysqli_result::fetch_array() mysqli_fetch_array()	Fetch a result row as an associative, a numeric array, or both
		mysqli_result::fetch_assoc() mysqli_fetch_assoc()	Fetch a result row as an associative array

*PHP 5.4 has MySQL native driver for PHP (mysqlnd) as default. As of PHP 5.4, the mysqlnd library is a php.net compile time default to all PHP MySQL extensions. Also, the php.net Windows team is using mysqlnd for the official PHP Windows distribution since mysqlnd became available in PHP 5.3.

2. Creating a Simple User Registration and Login Application

When you create a website where visitors to the site can become members or users of that website, you need to create a membership application or system that will handle the process of visitors joining your website. There are usually three parts to your user membership management system: registration, login and a protected member area. When visitors decide to become a member of your website, they must register with the site. At the minimum, this means they are creating a username and password and perhaps supplying you with their email address. Once a user has successfully registered and created an account, they can return to your site at any time and go through the login process to gain access to hidden or protected features of your website. This tutorial is going to teach you how to create a simple registration and login system using PHP and MySQL. You can, of course, add on more functionality or complexity to extend this simple system.

Note: **This recipe tutorial assumes that you, the reader, have some prior exposure to and familiarity with coding in PHP and SQL (Structured Query Language). The code in this tutorial may not include error checking. If you were to use this code in a production environment you should make your scripts secure and include error checking.**

2.1 Step 1: Creating the database or creating the User table

If you have not created a database that will hold the user information, create a database (from the MySQL database server command line, the control panel for your website account, or via a graphical frontend for MySQL etc.) and then create the user table from the code listed below. If you already have a database, proceed directly to creating a table. If using PHPMyAdmin as a graphical user interface (GUI) to interact with MySQL, you can copy and paste the SQL table creation code into PHPMyAdmin to create the user table.

SQL CODE

```
CREATE TABLE IF NOT EXISTS user (
  id int(4) UNSIGNED NOT NULL AUTO_INCREMENT,
  username varchar(32) NOT NULL DEFAULT "",
  password varchar(32) NOT NULL DEFAULT "",
  email varchar(100) NOT NULL DEFAULT "",
  level int(4) default '1',
  PRIMARY KEY  (id)
);
INSERT INTO user VALUES
('admin', 'adminpass', 'fake_admin_email@changeme.com', '9'),
('tester', 'testerpass', 'fake_tester_email@changeme.com', '9');
```

The SQL code above will create a table in your database called 'user.' The user table will have five columns/fields: id, username, password, email and level. The id is the unique primary key for the table and will be automatically assigned by the database. The username, password, and email fields will be populated from the information the user enters into the registration form.

The level column will allow your user management system to differentiate between users who are administrators (and therefore have more privileges) or regular users. The **default value is 1 for regular users** but if that value is changed to a different number that you assign, the user will become an administrator **i.e. if you change it to 9,**

the user will become an administrator. You must manually change this number in the user table for the user who will have admin privileges; otherwise the user level remains at 1 by default.

You should also consider collecting other information from new users such as a firstname and lastname. The user table could also store the date the user created the account and also keep track of the last time the user logged.

Note: This tutorial includes alternate SQL commands but does not also include alternate PHP code. The alternative is presented as a guide for further customizations that could be made to the application.

Alternate SQL

```
CREATE TABLE IF NOT EXISTS user (
 id int(4) UNSIGNED NOT NULL AUTO_INCREMENT,
 username varchar(32) NOT NULL DEFAULT "",
 password varchar(32) NOT NULL DEFAULT "",
 firstname varchar(100) DEFAULT NULL,
 lastname varchar(100) DEFAULT NULL,
 email varchar(100) NOT NULL DEFAULT "",
 registered datetime NOT NULL DEFAULT '0000-00-00 00:00:00',
 last_login datetime NOT NULL DEFAULT '0000-00-00 00:00:00',
 level int(4) default '1',
 PRIMARY KEY  (id)
);
```

2.2 Step 2: Creating the Registration Script

 The registration script – new members or users of your website will use this script to create/register new accounts.

"database.php"

CODE

MySQL

```php
<?php
// Connect to the database server. If a connection cannot
be made, an error will occur.
// Remember to fill in your username and password. Also
change 'localhost' if necessary.

$con = mysql_connect('localhost','root','password');
if (!$con)
  {
  die('Could not connect to MySQL server: ' .
mysql_error());
  } else{

// Select the database you want to use
//Remember to fill in your database name.
mysql_select_db('usersystem',$con) or die('Could not select
database: ' . mysql_error());

//echo "success";
  }
?>
```

Note: the "database.php" script is required. It opens a connection to the database.

MySQLi Procedural

```php
<?php
//Connect to the database server. If a connection can't be
made, an error will occur.
//Remember to, fill in your username and password. Also
change 'localhost' if necessary.

$con =
mysqli_connect('localhost','mysql_username','mysql_password
') or die(<p>The database server is not available.</p> ');
}

?>
```

MySQLi Object-Oriented

```php
<?php
$con = new
mysqli('localhost','mysql_username','mysql_password');

if($con->connect_errno > 0){
    die('Unable to connect to database [' . $con-
>connect_error . ']');
}
?>
```

PHP Data Object

```php
<?php
try{
```

```php
// example connecting to MySQL with the PDO extension
$con = new
PDO('mysql:host=localhost;dbname=usersystem','root','synod7
3');
// Set a PDO error mode
$con->setAttribute( PDO::ATTR_ERRMODE,
PDO::ERRMODE_EXCEPTION );
$con->exec('SET NAMES "utf8"');
}
catch(PDOException $e){
            echo 'Error connecting to MySQL!: '.$e-
>getMessage();
            exit();
}
?>
```

"reg.php"

CODE

```php
<?php
require_once 'database.php';
?>
<h1><strong>Register</strong></h1>
<form name="register" method="post" action="regcheck.php">
<label>
<input type="text" name="user" id="user">
</label>
Username <br><br>
<label>
<input type="password" name="pass" id="pass">
Password<br />
</label>
<label>
<input type="text" name="email" id="email" size="40">
</label>
<label>
<input type="submit" name="reg" id="reg" value="Register">
</label>
</form>
<p>
<form name="Back" method="post" action="login.php">
<label><input type="submit" name="back" id="back"
value="Back to Home"></label>
</form>
</p>
```

The reg.php script requires the "database.php" script, to open a connection to the database. The form collects the desired username and password from the new member, and also an email address.

Include() versus Require() functions

The **include()** function will output a warning if it cannot find a file i.e. database.php, but the PHP interpreter will attempt to execute the rest of your code; this is different behavior from the **require()** function, which will cause a fatal error and stop execution of a script if it cannot find a file or there is some other error with a file. When one script i.e. database.php is 'critical' to the correct functioning of another, stopping execution immediately is better versus allowing execution to continue until a later error is encountered in the including script. If the error messages outputted by the included script do not make the location very obvious, you could spend quite a bit of time looking for/attempting to fix errors in your main script that are caused by errors in the code of the script you included, and would disappear if the code in the other script was corrected.

2.3 Step 3: Checking for a Successful Registration

The registration check script, receives the user information for insertion into the user table via the $username, $password and $email variables passed from the form using the POST method. The script checks if the username, password and email fields were filled out. If they are, check if the fields are more than 5 characters and the email is in a valid email address format. Then check if the password is the same as the username. If no errors occurred, include/require the *database.php* script and insert the user information into the table.

Note: the password is md5 protected. You could also use the sha1() function to encrypt the password, or some other encryption function.

Things to consider about encryption

When you decide to encrypt the user password, you as the site administrator, has no knowledge of a user's password. As used in this script, the md5() function encrypts the password before it is inserted into the user table. This means you will not be able to plainly view the user's password, because it will be saved as an encrypted string of characters. When a user logs in, the password they entered is encrypted and that encrypted value is compared to the encrypted password value already stored in the user table.

You could alternatively, run an encryption function on password values when they are inserted into the user table i.e. INSERT INTO users (name, password) VALUES ('$name', **MD5('$password')**). In this scenario, you would not run a PHP md5() function on the $password variable before insertion into the user table, because the encryption would be handled by the MySQL server. The end result is still the same, an encrypted string of characters saved in the password field.

Typically, when passwords are stored in an encrypted format and a user management system has a 'forgot password/recover password' feature to send the user password via email, the user/administrator creates a new password. The system could be setup to automatically generate a new password or require the user to go to a specific page to create a new password. The new unencrypted password is sent in an email to the user while the new encrypted password value is stored in the database table.

** If you would like to give up the added security of encrypting user passwords, do not use an encryption function in PHP before inserting data, modify the script to remove the md5() function i.e. '$password = $_POST['pass'];' and do not use one in SQL insertion statements.

"regcheck.php"

CODE

MySQL

```php
<?php
// some error checking
/*
if($_POST['reg']){
echo "form submitted";
}else{ echo "form not submitted"; }
*/

if( isset( $_POST['user'] ) && isset( $_POST['pass'] ) &&
isset( $_POST['email'] ) ){
    // echo $_POST['user']." - ".$_POST['pass']." -
".$_POST['email'];

    if( strlen( $_POST['user'] ) < 5 )
    {
        include('header.inc');
        echo "Username Must Be More Than 5 Characters.";
        include('footer.inc');
```

```php
    }
    elseif( strlen( $_POST['pass'] ) < 5 )
    {
        include('header.inc');
        echo "Password Must Be More Than 5 Characters.";
        include('footer.inc');
    }
    elseif( $_POST['pass'] == $_POST['user'] )
    {
        include('header.inc');
        echo "Username And Password Can Not Be The Same.";
        include('footer.inc');
    }
  elseif( $_POST['email'] == "" )
    {
        //More secure to use a regular expression to check
that the user is entering a valid email
        // versus just checking to see if the field is
empty
        include('header.inc');
        echo "Email must be valid.";
        include('footer.inc');
    }
    else
    {
        require( 'database.php' );

        $username = mysql_real_escape_string(
$_POST['user'] );

        //Remove md5() function if not using encryption
i.e. $password = $_POST['pass'];
        $password = md5( $_POST['pass'] );

        $email = mysql_real_escape_string( $_POST['email']
);

        $sqlCheckForDuplicate = "SELECT username FROM user
WHERE username = '". $username ."'";
```

```php
        if( mysql_num_rows( mysql_query(
$sqlCheckForDuplicate ) ) == 0 )
        {
            $sqlRegUser =       "INSERT INTO
                        user( username, password, email )
                    VALUES(
                        '". $username ."',
                        '". $password ."',
                        '". $email."'
                        )";
            //echo "$sqlRegUser";

            if( !mysql_query( $sqlRegUser ) )
            {
                include('header.inc');
                echo "You Could Not Register Because Of An
Unexpected Error.";
                include('footer.inc');
            }
            else
            {
/* Note: When using the header function, you cannot send
output * to the browser before the header function is
called. IF you
* want to echo a message to the user before going back to
your
* login page then you should use the HTML Meta Refresh tag.
*/

 //echo "You Are Registered And Can Now Login";
//echo " $username;"  //this is for error checking

   header ('location: login.php');

// if using echo then use meta refresh
/*
 *?>
 *<meta http-equiv="refresh" content="2;url= login.php/">
```

```
*<?
*/



                }
          }
          else
          {
                include('header.inc');
                echo "The Username You Have Chosen Is Already
Being Used By Another User. Please Try Another One.";
                //echo " $username;"   //this is for error
checking
                include('footer.inc');
          }
     }
}
else
{
     include('header.inc');
     echo "You Could Not Be Registered Because Of Missing
Data.";
     include('footer.inc');
}
?>
```

Alternate SQL

```
$sqlRegUser = "INSERT INTO user( username, password,
firstname, lastname, email, registered, last_login)
VALUES('". $username ."','". $password ."','". $email."',
NOW(), NOW() )";
```

The regcheck.php also checks if a username already exists, if it does not, the account will be registered, and the user will be redirected to the *login.php* page (this could also be any other page i.e. index.php). But if a username is already taken, the script will inform the user attempting to register that the username is being used and prompt to choose another name.

MySQLi Procedural

```php
<?php
error_reporting(E_ALL);
ini_set('display_errors', '1');

// some error checking
/*
if($_POST['reg']){
echo "form submitted";
}else{ echo "form not submitted"; }
*/

if( isset( $_POST['user'] ) && isset( $_POST['pass'] ) &&
isset( $_POST['email'] ) ){
    // echo $_POST['user']." - ".$_POST['pass']." -
".$_POST['email'];

    if( strlen( $_POST['user'] ) < 5 )
    {
        include('header.inc');
        echo "Username Must Be More Than 5 Characters.";
        include('footer.inc');
    }
    elseif( strlen( $_POST['pass'] ) < 5 )
    {
        include('header.inc');
        echo "Password Must Be More Than 5 Characters.";
        include('footer.inc');
    }
    elseif( $_POST['pass'] == $_POST['user'] )
    {
        include('header.inc');
        echo "Username And Password Can Not Be The Same.";
        include('footer.inc');
    }
  elseif( $_POST['email'] == "" )
```

```php
    {
        //More secure to use a regular expression to check
that the user is entering a valid email
        // versus just checking to see if the field is
empty
        include('header.inc');
        echo "Email must be valid.";
        include('footer.inc');
    }
    else
    {

        require( 'database.php' );

        $username = mysqli_real_escape_string($con,
$_POST['user']);

        //Remove md5() function if not using encryption
i.e. $password = $_POST['pass'];
        $password = mysqli_real_escape_string($con, md5(
$_POST['pass']));

        $email = mysqli_real_escape_string($con,
$_POST['email'] );

        $sqlCheckForDuplicate = "SELECT username FROM user
WHERE username = '". $username ."'";
        //echo "$sqlCheckForDuplicate<br/>";

        $result = mysqli_query($con,
$sqlCheckForDuplicate);

        if(mysqli_num_rows($result) == 0){

           //echo "No Duplicates<br/>";

           $sqlRegUser = "INSERT INTO user( username,
password, email ) VALUES (
                       '". $username ."',
```

```
                              '". $password ."',
                              '". $email."'
                              )";
            //echo "$sqlRegUser<br/>";

            if( !mysqli_query($con, $sqlRegUser ) )
              {
                   include('header.inc');
                   echo "You Could Not Register Because Of An
Unexpected Error.";
                   include('footer.inc');
              }

              else
              {
/* Note: When using the header function, you cannot send
output * to the browser before the header function is
called. IF you
* want to echo a message to the user before going back to
your
* login page then you should use the HTML Meta Refresh tag.
*/

 //echo "You Are Registered And Can Now Login";
 //echo " $username";   //this is for error checking

   header ('location: login.php');

// if using echo then use meta refresh
/*
 *?>
 *<meta http-equiv="refresh" content="2;url= login.php/">
 *<?
 */

              }
        mysqli_free_result($result);

        }
```

```php
        else
        {
            include('header.inc');
            echo "The Username You Have Chosen Is Already
Being Used By Another User. Please Try Another One.";
            //echo " $username;"   //this is for error
checking
            include('footer.inc');
        }
        /* close connection */
        mysqli_close($con);
    }
}
else
{
    include('header.inc');
    echo "You Could Not Be Registered Because Of Missing
Data.";
    include('footer.inc');
}
?>
```

MySQLi Object-Oriented

```php
<?php
error_reporting(E_ALL);

ini_set('display_errors', '1');

// some error checking
/*
if($_POST['reg']){
echo "form submitted";
}else{ echo "form not submitted"; }
*/

if( isset( $_POST['user'] ) && isset( $_POST['pass'] ) &&
isset( $_POST['email'] ) ){
    // echo $_POST['user']." - ".$_POST['pass']." -
".$_POST['email'];

    if( strlen( $_POST['user'] ) < 5 )
    {
        include('header.inc');
        echo "Username Must Be More Than 5 Characters.";
        include('footer.inc');
    }
    elseif( strlen( $_POST['pass'] ) < 5 )
    {
        include('header.inc');
        echo "Password Must Be More Than 5 Characters.";
        include('footer.inc');
    }
    elseif( $_POST['pass'] == $_POST['user'] )
    {
        include('header.inc');
        echo "Username And Password Can Not Be The Same.";
        include('footer.inc');
    }
  elseif( $_POST['email'] == "" )
```

```php
    {
        //More secure to use a regular expression to check
that the user is entering a valid email
        // versus just checking to see if the field is
empty
        include('header.inc');
        echo "Email must be valid.";
        include('footer.inc');
    }
    else
    {

        require( 'database.php' );

        $username = mysqli_real_escape_string($con,
$_POST['user']);

        //Remove md5() function if not using encryption
i.e. $password = $_POST['pass'];
        $password = mysqli_real_escape_string($con, md5(
$_POST['pass']));

        $email = mysqli_real_escape_string($con,
$_POST['email'] );

        $sqlCheckForDuplicate = "SELECT username FROM user
WHERE username = '". $username ."'";
            //echo "$sqlCheckForDuplicate<br/>";

        $result = mysqli_query($con,
$sqlCheckForDuplicate);

        if(mysqli_num_rows($result) == 0){

          //echo "No Duplicates<br/>";

          $sqlRegUser = "INSERT INTO user( username,
password, email ) VALUES (
                        '". $username ."',
```

```php
                        '". $password ."',
                        '". $email."'
                        )";
            //echo "$sqlRegUser<br/>";

         if( !mysqli_query($con, $sqlRegUser ) )
            {
                 include('header.inc');
                 echo "You Could Not Register Because Of An
Unexpected Error.";
                 include('footer.inc');
            }

            else
            {
/* Note: When using the header function, you cannot send
output * to the browser before the header function is
called. IF you
* want to echo a message to the user before going back to
your
* login page then you should use the HTML Meta Refresh tag.
*/

 //echo "You Are Registered And Can Now Login";
 //echo " $username";  //this is for error checking

    header ('location: login.php');

// if using echo then use meta refresh
/*
 *?>
 *<meta http-equiv="refresh" content="2;url= login.php/">
 *<?
 */

            }
        mysqli_free_result($result);

        }
```

```
        else
        {
            include('header.inc');
            echo "The Username You Have Chosen Is Already
Being Used By Another User. Please Try Another One.";
            //echo " $username;"  //this is for error
checking
            include('footer.inc');
        }
        /* close connection */
        mysqli_close($con);
        }
    }
else
{
    include('header.inc');
    echo "You Could Not Be Registered Because Of Missing
Data.";
    include('footer.inc');
}
?>
```

OUTPUT

Register

Username: [   ]

Password: [   ]

Email: [   ] [Register]

[Back to Home]

PHP Data Object

```php
<?php

error_reporting(E_ALL);
ini_set('display_errors', '1');

// some error checking
/*
if($_POST['reg']){
echo "form submitted";
}else{ echo "form not submitted"; }
*/

if( isset( $_POST['user'] ) && isset( $_POST['pass'] ) &&
isset( $_POST['email'] ) ){
    // echo $_POST['user']." - ".$_POST['pass']." -
".$_POST['email'];

    if( strlen( $_POST['user'] ) < 5 )
    {
        include('header.inc');
        echo "Username Must Be More Than 5 Characters.";
        include('footer.inc');
    }
    elseif( strlen( $_POST['pass'] ) < 5 )
    {
        include('header.inc');
        echo "Password Must Be More Than 5 Characters.";
        include('footer.inc');
    }
    elseif( $_POST['pass'] == $_POST['user'] )
    {
        include('header.inc');
        echo "Username And Password Can Not Be The Same.";
        include('footer.inc');
    }
```

```php
    elseif(!filter_var($_POST['email'],
FILTER_VALIDATE_EMAIL))
    {
        //FILTER_VALIDATE_EMAIL filter validates value as
an e-mail address.
        include('header.inc');
        echo "Email must be valid.";
        include('footer.inc');
    }
    else
    {
        require( 'database.php' );

        $username = $_POST['user'];

        //Remove md5() function if not using encryption
i.e. $password = $_POST['pass'];
        $password = md5( $_POST['pass'] );

        $email = $_POST['email'];

        try{
        $sqlCheckForDuplicate = "SELECT username FROM
user WHERE username = ?";
        //sqlCheckForDuplicate = "SELECT username FROM
user WHERE username = :username ";

        $stmt = $con->prepare($sqlCheckForDuplicate);

        $stmt->bindParam(1, $username);
        //$stmt->bindParam(":username", $username);

        $stmt->execute();
        $dupCount = $stmt->fetch();
        }
        catch (PDOException $e)
        {
          $error = 'Error: ' . $e->getMessage();
            echo $error;
```

```php
        exit();
    }

    if ($dupCount[0] == 0)
    {

    try{
        $sqlRegUser =   "INSERT INTO user ( username,
password, email ) VALUES (?,?,?)";
        //$sqlRegUser =   "INSERT INTO user ( username,
password, email ) VALUES ( :username, :password, :email )";

        $stmt = $con->prepare($sqlRegUser);
        $stmt->bindParam(1, $username);
        $stmt->bindParam(2, $password);
            $stmt->bindParam(3, $email);

            //$stmt->bindParam(":username", $username);
        //$stmt->bindParam(":password", $password);
            //$stmt->bindParam(":email", $email);

            //Note if you need to insert a null value
            //$stmt->bindValue(':param', null,
PDO::PARAM_INT);
            //or $stmt->bindValue(':param', null,
PDO::PARAM_NULL);
            //or try
            //$valnull = PDO::PARAM_NULL;
            //$stmt->bindParam(':param', $valnull);

        $stmt->execute();

        $count = $stmt->rowCount();

        if( $count < 1 ){
            // Problem Creating User
            include('header.inc');
            echo "You Could Not Register Because Of An
Unexpected Error.";
```

```
            include('footer.inc');
        }else{
            // New User Account Created

/* Note: When using the header function, you cannot send
output to the browser
* before the header function is called. IF you want to echo
a message to the
* user before going back to your login page then you should
use the HTML
* Meta Refresh tag. */

    //echo "You Are Registered And Can Now Login";
    //echo " $username";  //this is for error checking

            header ('location: login.php');

    // if using echo then use meta refresh
    /*
     *?>
     *<meta http-equiv="refresh" content="2;url=
login.php/">
     *<?
     */

            }

                }
        catch (PDOException $e)
        {
          $error = 'Error: ' . $e->getMessage();
              echo $error;
              exit();
        }

        }
        else
        {
            include('header.inc');
```

```php
            echo "The Username You Have Chosen Is Already
Being Used By Another User. Please Try Another One.";
            //echo " $username;"  //this is for error
checking
            include('footer.inc');
        }

    /* close connection */
            $con = null;

    }
}
else
{
    include('header.inc');
    echo "You Could Not Be Registered Because Of Missing
Data.";
    include('footer.inc');
}
?>
```

2.4 Step 4: Login

The **login.php** script checks to see if the login form was submitted by the user. If the form has been submitted then execute the loginUser() function and redirect or output a message to the user on successful login. If the form has not been submitted, the script will display the form. By organizing the script in this manner, the login form only shows up when needed. This script uses sessions to keep track of state. Call session_start() at the beginning of your scripts to either start a session or continue using session variables set on other pages.

"login.php"

CODE

MySQL

```php
<?php
session_start();  //this will start the session for the
user

require( 'database.php' );

if ( isset( $_POST['login']) ) {
        loginUser();
    } else {

include('header.inc');
?>
    <form action="<?=$_SERVER['PHP_SELF']; ?>"
method="POST">
    Username: <input type="text" name="username"><br>
    Password: <input type="password" name="password"><br>
    <input type="submit" name="login" value="Login">
  </form>
```

```php
<?php

include('footer.inc');
}

    function loginUser() {
    $username = $_POST['username'];
    $password = md5($_POST['password']);

    //echo "$username - $password";

    $sql = "SELECT user.id, username, password FROM user
WHERE username = '$username' AND password = '$password' AND
level='1'";   // This statement will check if the user is a
level 1 user (Normal User)
//echo "$sql";

    $sql2 = "SELECT user.id, username, password FROM user
WHERE username = '$username' AND password = '$password' AND
level='9'";   // This statement will check if the user is a
level 9 user (Admin User)

//echo "$sql2";

/*
Note: Depending on the setup of your server, you may need
to modify your SQL statements to similar to the statements
below
    $sql = "SELECT user.id, username, password FROM user
WHERE username = '".$username."' AND password =
'".$password."' AND level='1'";

    $sql2 = "SELECT user.id, username, password FROM user
WHERE username = '".$username."' AND password =
'".$password."' AND level='9'";
*/

    $result = mysql_query($sql);
    $result2 = mysql_query($sql2);
```

```php
if(mysql_num_rows($result) > 0){

    $row = mysql_fetch_assoc($result);

    if ($row) {
        $_SESSION['loggedin'] = 1;
        $_SESSION['loggedinuser'] = $row['username'];
        $_SESSION['adminuser'] = 0;   //not an admin set
value to false/0

        //Decide what to do with the user once s/he is
logged in
        //Output a message, navigation menu, redirect to
another page etc.
        include('header.inc');
        //echo "Logged In, {$row['username']}";
        echo "Logged In, {$_SESSION['loggedinuser']}";
        echo "<p>This is to demonstrate regular protected
page behavior to users not logged in <a href=\"
protected_page.php\">Protected page</a></p>";
        echo "<p>This is to demonstrate admin protected page
behavior for regular users <a
href=\"protected_admin_page.php\">Protected admin
page</a></p>";
        echo "<p><a href=\"logout.php\">Logout</a></p>";
        include('footer.inc');
    }

}
elseif (mysql_num_rows($result2) > 0){

    $row2 = mysql_fetch_assoc($result2);

    if ($row2) {
        $_SESSION['loggedin'] = 1;
        $_SESSION['loggedinuser'] = $row2['username'];
        $_SESSION['adminuser'] = 1; //yes is an admin set
value to true/1
```

```php
        //Decide what to do with the user once s/he is
logged in
        //Output a message, navigation menu, redirect to
another page etc.
        include('header.inc');
        //echo "Logged In, {$row2['username']}, as admin";
        echo "Logged In, {$_SESSION['loggedinuser']}, as
admin";
        echo "<p><a href=\"protected_page.php\">Protected
regular user page</a></p>";
        echo "<p><a
href=\"protected_admin_page.php\">Protected admin
page</a></p>";
        echo "<p><a href=\"logout.php\">Logout</a></p>";
        include('footer.inc');
    }
}
// decide what to do if the login is unsuccessful
else{
include('header.inc');
echo "There was a problem with your login. It Could be the
Wrong Username or Password";
include('footer.inc');
}

} // end function
?>
```

MySQLi Procedural

```php
<?php
session_start();  //this will start the session for the
user

error_reporting(E_ALL);
ini_set('display_errors', '1');

require( 'database.php' );

if ( isset( $_POST['login']) ) {
        loginUser($con);
    } else {

include('header.inc');
?>
    <form action="<?php echo $_SERVER['PHP_SELF']; ?>"
method="POST">
    Username: <input type="text" name="username"><br>
   Password: <input type="password" name="password"><br>
   <input type="submit" name="login" value="Login">
  </form>
 <?php

 include('footer.inc');
 }

function loginUser($con) {
   $username = mysqli_real_escape_string($con,
$_POST['username']);
   $password = mysqli_real_escape_string($con,
md5($_POST['password']));

   //echo "$username - $password";
```

```php
    $sql = "SELECT user.id, username, password, level FROM
user WHERE username = '$username' AND password =
'$password'";
    //echo "$sql";

/*
Note: Depending on the setup of your server, you may need
to modify your SQL statements to similar to the statements
below
    $sql = "SELECT user.id, username, password FROM user
WHERE username = '".$username."' AND password =
'".$password."' AND level='1'";
 */

$result = mysqli_query($con, $sql);

if(mysqli_num_rows($result) > 0){

    $row = mysqli_fetch_assoc($result);

    if ($row) {
        //echo "Reached Matching Row<br/>";

        $_SESSION['loggedin'] = 1;
        $_SESSION['loggedinuser'] = $row['username'];

        if($row['level'] == '1'){   //level 1 user (Normal
User)

            //echo "Reached level 1 check<br/>";

        //not an admin set value to false/0
$_SESSION['adminuser'] = 0;

        header ('location: main.php');
}
        //level 9 user (Admin User)
elseif ($row['level'] == '9'){
```

```php
        //echo "Reached level 9 check<br/>";

        //yes is an admin set value to true/1
$_SESSION['adminuser'] = 1;

        header ('location: main.php');

}
    }
    mysqli_free_result($result);
}
// decide what to do if the login is unsuccessful
else{
include('header.inc');
echo "There was a problem with your login. It Could be the
Wrong Username or Password";
include('footer.inc');
}

} // end function

/* close connection */
mysqli_close($con);

?>
```

MySQLi Object-Oriented

```php
<?php
session_cache_limiter('private_no_expire');  //same as
calling ini_set('session.cache_limiter','private')
//session_cache_limiter ('private_no_expire, must-
revalidate');

session_start();  //this will start the session for the
user

date_default_timezone_set("America/New_York");

error_reporting(E_ALL);
ini_set('display_errors', '1');

require( 'database_oo.php' );

if ( isset( $_POST['login']) ) {
        loginUser($con);
    } else {

include('header.inc');
?>

    <form action="<?php echo $_SERVER['PHP_SELF']; ?>"
method="POST">
    Username: <input type="text" name="username"><br>
    Password: <input type="password" name="password"><br>
    <input type="submit" name="login" value="Login">
    </form>

<?php

  include('footer.inc');
  }
```

```php
function loginUser($con) {  //You must pass the $con
variable (assuming that is what your mysqli connection is
in) into your function as a parameter when you call the
function

$username = $con->real_escape_string($_POST['username']);
$password = $con-
>real_escape_string(md5($_POST['password']));

   //echo "$username - $password";

   $sql = "SELECT user.id, username, password, level FROM
user WHERE username = '$username' AND password =
'$password'";
    //echo "$sql";

   /*
   Note: Depending on the setup of your server, you may
need to modify your SQL statements to similar to the
statements below
   $sql = "SELECT user.id, username, password FROM user
WHERE username = '".$username."' AND password =
'".$password."' AND level='1'";
   */

   $result = $con->query($sql);

   /*
   if ($result){
     echo "<p>Found Row</p>";
   } else {
     echo('Problem: '. $con->connect_errno() .' :: '. $con-
>connect_error());
     echo "<p>Your query returned " .
   $result->num_rows . " rows and "
        . $result->num_fields . " fields.</p>";
   }
   */
```

```php
if($result->num_rows > 0){

    $row = $result->fetch_assoc();

    if ($row) {
      //echo "Reached Matching Row<br/>";

        $_SESSION['loggedin'] = 1;
        $_SESSION['loggedinuser'] = $row['username'];

         //level 1 user (Normal User)
if($row['level'] == '1'){

//echo "Reached level 1 check<br/>";

        //not an admin set value to false/0
$_SESSION['adminuser'] = 0;

        header ('location: main.php');
}
        //level 9 user (Admin User)
elseif ($row['level'] == '9'){

        //echo "Reached level 9 check<br/>";

        //yes is an admin set value to true/1
$_SESSION['adminuser'] = 1;

        header ('location: main.php');
}

    }
    $result->free_result();
}

// decide what to do if the login is unsuccessful

else{
include('header.inc');
```

```
echo "There was a problem with your login. It Could be the
Wrong Username or Password";
include('footer.inc');
}

} // end function

/* close connection */
$con->close();
?>
```

OUTPUT

Username: |

Password:

[Login]

PHP Data Object

```php
<?php
session_start();  //this will start the session for the
user

error_reporting(E_ALL);
ini_set('display_errors', '1');

require( 'database.php' );

if ( isset( $_POST['login']) ) {
        loginUser($con);
    } else {

include('header.inc');
?>
    <form action="<?php echo $_SERVER['PHP_SELF']; ?>"
method="POST">
    Username: <input type="text" name="username"><br>
   Password: <input type="password" name="password"><br>
   <input type="submit" name="login" value="Login">
  </form>
 <?php

 include('footer.inc');
 }

function loginUser($con) {
$username = $_POST['username'];
$password = md5($_POST['password']);

//echo "$username - $password";

$sql = "SELECT user.id, username, password, level FROM user
WHERE username = ? AND password = ?";
```

```php
// alternate statement: $sql = "SELECT user.id, username,
password, level FROM user WHERE username = :username AND
password = :password";

try{
$stmt = $con->prepare($sql);

$stmt->bindParam(1, $username);
$stmt->bindParam(2, $password);

// alternate statement: $stmt->bindParam(":username",
$username);
// alternate statement: $stmt->bindParam(":password",
$password);

// Setting the PDO fetch method
$stmt->setFetchMode(PDO::FETCH_ASSOC);
$stmt->execute();


/*
Note: If you are using a MySQL database,
PDOStatement::rowCount returns the number of rows in a
SELECT result set. But you should not depend on this
behavior when using other databases.

Generally, 'PDOStatement::rowCount() returns the number of
rows affected by the last DELETE, INSERT, or UPDATE
statement executed by the corresponding PDOStatement
object. If the last SQL statement executed by the
associated PDOStatement was a SELECT statement, some
databases may return the number of rows returned by that
statement. However, this behaviour is not guaranteed for
all databases and should not be relied on for portable
applications.'
*/

$total = $stmt->rowCount();
```

```php
if($total > 0){

    if($row = $stmt->fetch()) {

        $_SESSION['loggedin'] = 1;
        $_SESSION['loggedinuser'] = $row['username'];

    if($row['level'] == '1'){
     //level 1 user (Normal User)
      //echo "Reached level 1 check<br/>";

        $_SESSION['adminuser'] = 0;
        //not an admin set value to false/0
        header ('location: main.php');
    }
        elseif ($row['level'] == '9'){
          //level 9 user (Admin User)
          //echo "Reached level 9 check<br/>";

        $_SESSION['adminuser'] = 1;
         //yes is an admin set value to true/1
        header ('location: main.php');
    }

    // Close the cursor
    /* The following call to closeCursor() may be required
by some drivers */
    $stmt->closeCursor();
    }
  }
// decide what to do if the login is unsuccessful
else{
include('header.inc');
echo "There was a problem with your login. It Could be the
Wrong Username or Password";
include('footer.inc');
}

}  // end try
```

```php
catch (PDOException $e)
{
$error = 'Error: ' . $e->getMessage();
    echo $error;
    exit();
}

} // end function

/* close connection */
    $con = null;
?>
```

2.5 Step 5: Protected Pages or Areas

After successfully logging into the membership system, the login script redirects the user to a main or homepage area. On this page you would provide links to other controlled access pages or actions that could be performed as a logged in user. If a user is not logged in, you would typically block the user from viewing certain pages until s/he logs into the system. When a user logs in, you check their level of access. This system has two levels: administrators and regular user. Perhaps there will be pages that only administrators will be able to view. When a visitor or user tries to access a page with controlled access, you could output an error message, or direct the visitor/user to register or login.

On **any PHP page you want to protect**, check the already started session to see if the user is logged in. If the user is not logged in, decide on an action. In this example the script stops execution to ouput an error message. Remember when using sessions that the session_start() function must be called immediately after the opening PHP tag.

"main.php"

CODE

```
<?php
session_start();  //this will start the session for the
user

error_reporting(E_ALL);
ini_set('display_errors', '1');

if (!isset($_SESSION['loggedin'])) {
```

```php
    die("Not logged in"); //this causes to script to stop
executing and lets the user know there is a problem


/*

Note:  instead of the die() function, you could use the
echo() function and provide an HTML link back to the login
page, or use the header() function to just redirect users
to the login page without any message. It is up to you to
decide how your application should function.

*/

}


elseif (isset($_SESSION['loggedin']) &&
($_SESSION['adminuser']=='0') ){  //logged in and NOT an
Admin


        //Decide what to do with the user once s/he is
logged in
        //Output a message, navigation menu, redirect to
another page etc.
        include('header.inc');
        echo "Logged in as:
{$_SESSION['loggedinuser']}<br/><br/>\n";
        echo "<p>This is to demonstrate regular protected
page behavior to regular  users logged in <a
href=\"protected_page.php\">Protected page</a></p>";
        echo "<p>This is to demonstrate admin protected page
behavior for regular users <a
href=\"protected_admin_page.php\">Protected admin
page</a></p>";
        echo "<p><a href=\"logout.php\">Logout</a></p>";
        include('footer.inc');
```

```php
        }


elseif (isset($_SESSION['loggedin']) &&
($_SESSION['adminuser']=='1') ){  //logged in and an Admin


/* what a user would be able to do if logged in and the
Admin. It is up to you to decide how your application
should function. */


        //Decide what to do with the user once s/he is
logged in
        //Output a message, navigation menu, redirect to
another page etc.
        include('header.inc');
        echo "Logged in as: {$_SESSION['loggedinuser']} -
[ADMIN]<br/><br/>\n";
        echo "<p><a href=\"protected_page.php\">Protected
regular user page</a></p>";
        echo "<p><a
href=\"protected_admin_page.php\">Protected admin
page</a></p>";
        echo "<p><a href=\"logout.php\">Logout</a></p>";
        include('footer.inc');
}
?>
```

The **"main.php"** displays slightly different text based on the user level. It checks to see if the logged in user is, or is not, an admin level user. This page is a good checkpoint to make sure you have setup your permission levels in your database table and coded your authentication logic correctly; login and logut, as different level users, to test that this page (or any of the other 'protected' pages) are functioning correctly. If a user is able to access a page they should not have access to or they cannot access a page they should be able to access, there is obviously a problem.

"protected_page.php"

CODE

```php
<?php
session_start();

if (!$_SESSION['loggedin']) {
die("Not logged in"); //this causes the script to stop
executing and lets the user know there is a problem

/*
Note: instead of the die() function, you could use the
echo() function and provide an HTML link back to the login
page, or use the header() function to just redirect users
to the login page without any message. It is up to you to
decide how your application should function.
*/
}
else{
/* what a user would be able to do if logged in. It is up
to you to decide how your application should function. */
echo "<p>Logged in as: {$_SESSION['loggedinuser']} </p>";

echo "<p><a href=\"memberlist.php\">Membership
List</a></p>";
echo "<p><a href=\"logout.php\">Logout</a></p>";}
?>
```

*** On **any other PHP page you want to protect** and ONLY the ADMIN will have access to, not only do you check if the user is logged in, you must also **check to see if the user is an admin**.

"**protected_admin_page.php**"

CODE

```php
<?php
session_start();
if (!$_SESSION['loggedin']) {
die("Not logged in"); //this causes the script to stop
executing and lets the user know there is a problem

/*
Note: instead of the die() function, you could use the
echo() function and provide an HTML link back to the login
page, or use the header() function to just redirect users
to the login page without any message. It is up to you to
decide how your application should function.
*/
}

elseif ($_SESSION['loggedin'] &&
($_SESSION['adminuser']=='0') ){  //logged in and NOT an
Admin
die("You do not have the right privileges to access this
page");
}

elseif ($_SESSION['loggedin'] &&
($_SESSION['adminuser']=='1') ){  //logged in and an Admin

/* what a user would be able to do if logged in and the
Admin. It is up to you to decide how your application
should function. */

echo "<p>Logged in as: {$_SESSION['loggedinuser']} -
[ADMIN]</p>";

echo "<p><a href=\"admin.php\">Administer Members
List</a></p>";
```

```php
echo "<p><a href=\"logout.php\">Logout</a></p>";

}
?>
```

2.6 Step 6: Logout

When the user is done using your application it needs to log them out and remove any session information stored about the user. You can use the session_unset() and session_destroy() functions to accomplish this. **Start the session, remove all session data, with session_unset and session_destroy.** Once the session information is destroyed, you could redirect the user back to the login page, some other page or output a suggestion. In this case, the script prints a link to the login page.

"logout.php"

CODE

```php
<?php
session_start();   //This will start the session
session_unset();   //Session_unset will remove any session
variables set
session_destroy();   //Session_destroy will remove the
session

//header("location:login.php");   //Redirect back to the
login/index page

echo "Logged Out";
echo "<p><a href=\"login.php\">Login Again</a></p>";

?>
```

3. Design

As you read through the example scripts, pay attention to their use of inline styling on the HTML elements. Correct practice would be to remove all styling to an external Cascading Style Sheet or between style tags in the header section of the HTML produced by your scripts. You can use a header.inc and a footer.inc file to contain your HTML design.

If you have an overall page designed, with a header, content area and footer, you can split that page into three sections. The header file would have the top portion or header of a page with HTML/CSS/JavaScript and perhaps any sidebars. The main PHP script that includes the header and footer files, should be coded to output into the content area of the overall page. The footer file would contain the footer portion of the page. Use the include() function to include the files where needed. You can also use the require() function.

Possible div layout:

Header	
Menu/Sidebar	**Body/Content**
Footer	

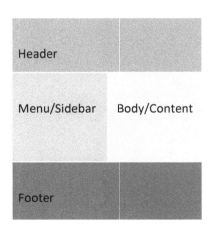

Header
Body/Content
Footer

CODE SNIPPET

```
include('header.inc');

//more PHP code here to produce content divs

include('footer.inc');
```

4. Extending the User Login Application

There are many ways you can build on or extend the application. Beyond having a user registration membership system, what does your website do? What does the website provide for users?

Examples of website services:

If the website is a gallery, perhaps registered users can upload their own gallery images and vote on other user images.

If the website is a forum, users can start discussion and contribute comments to discussions.

If the website is a social network, users can connect with friends, join groups, play games etc.

If it is an e-commerce website, users can purchase goods and store their payment information for the next time they want to buy.

The extension provided with this application is a membership list and profile page. Registered users will be able to view a list of all the members/users of your application/website. The list of names will act as individual links to a member profile page that will display more detailed information for each user. The selected link passes the user id to the profile page, pulling out the full user details. As an administrator, this profile page can also act as the page where you delete individual user accounts, by including a delete button. By adding on additional features, these two scripts can serve as the building blocks of the administrative backend for this application.

4.1 Step 1: Creating the Membership List Script

The membership list script – a simple list of the members or users of your website. The script will select all the records from the table which stores the user information, in this case the table is named 'users'. These records can be ordered by ID; which will order by the unique id number assigned when users registered. Alternatively, records can be ordered by another ordering method, such as ordering by USERNAME, which would place the users in an alphabetical list.

Suggested SQL

```
$result = mysqli_query($con, "SELECT * FROM user ORDER BY id");
```
or
```
$result = mysqli_query($con, "SELECT * FROM user ORDER BY username");
```

"memberlist.php"

CODE

MySQL

```php
<?php
session_start();

date_default_timezone_set("America/New_York");

error_reporting(E_ALL);
ini_set('display_errors', '1');

require( 'database.php' );

if (!$_SESSION['loggedin']) {
```

```php
    die("Not logged in"); //this causes the script to stop
executing and lets the user know there is a problem

/*
Note: instead of the die() function, you could use the
echo() function and provide an HTML link back to the login
page, or use the header() function to just redirect users
to the login page without any message. It is up to you to
decide how your application should function.
*/
}

//else {   //logged in
elseif (isset($_SESSION['loggedin']) ){   //logged in

/* what a user would be able to do if logged in. It is up
to you to decide how your application should function. */

echo "Logged in as: {$_SESSION['loggedinuser']} ";
if ($_SESSION['adminuser']=='1'){ echo "- [ADMIN]";}
echo "<br/><br/>";

//Set this to the number of records per page
$limit = 5;

if(isset($_GET['offset'])){
$offset=$_GET['offset'];
}
else{

//Set the initial offset
if (!isset($offset)) $offset = 0;
}

$offset = mysql_real_escape_string($offset);
$limit = mysql_real_escape_string($limit);

$result = mysql_query("SELECT * FROM user ORDER BY username
LIMIT $offset, $limit");
```

```
$result_total = mysql_query("SELECT * FROM user");
$totalcount = mysql_num_rows($result_total);


echo "<br/>";
print("There are currently <b>$totalcount</b> Users.");
print("<br/><br/>\n");

echo "<table border='0'><tr>
<th>Username</th>
</tr>";

while($row = mysql_fetch_array($result))
{
echo "<tr>";
printf ("<td><a href=\"profile.php?uid=%s\">%s</a></td>",
$row['id'], $row['username']);
echo "</tr>";
}
echo "</table><br/>";

//print the links created by the navigation function
print get_nav($offset, $limit, $totalcount);

echo "<p><a href=\"main.php\">Back to Main page</a></p>";
echo "<p><a href=\"logout.php\">Logout</a></p>";

}

function get_nav($offset, $limit, $totalnum) {
$navigation ='';

/* based the limit set for the number of records to show,
and the total number of records found, this function
calculates how many next, previous and page links to create
for navigation */

if ($totalnum > $limit) {
$navigation .= sprintf('<table><tr><td>');
```

```php
// Print Record # - # of # (Customize to your need here)
$navigation  .= sprintf('Record(s) %s', ( $offset + 1 ));
$navigation  .= sprintf(' - ');
if( $offset + $limit >= $totalnum ){
$navigation  .= sprintf($totalnum);
}else{ $navigation  .= sprintf ( $offset + $limit ); }
$navigation  .= sprintf(' of %s    |   </td>', $totalnum);

$navigation .= sprintf('<td>Page </td>',"\n");

//print previous
if ($offset != 0) {
$boffset = $offset-$limit;
$navigation .= sprintf('<td><a
href="%s?offset=%s"><<</a></td>',$_SERVER['PHP_SELF'],$boff
set);
}

// calculate number of pages needing links
$pages = intval($totalnum/$limit);

// $pages now contains int of pages needed unless there is
a remainder from division
if ($totalnum%$limit) $pages++;

//print pages
for ($i=1; $i <= $pages; $i++) {  // loop thru
$newoffset=$limit*($i-1);
if ($newoffset != $offset) {
$navigation .= sprintf('<td><a
href="%s?offset=%s">%s</a></td>%s',
$_SERVER['PHP_SELF'], $newoffset, $i, "\n");
}
else {
$navigation .= sprintf('<td>%s</td>%s', $i, "\n");
}
}
```

```php
//print next
$noffset = $pages*$limit-$limit;
if ($offset != $noffset)
{
$boffset = $offset+$limit;
$navigation .= sprintf('<td><a
href="%s?offset=%s">>></a></td>',
$_SERVER['PHP_SELF'], $boffset);
}

$navigation .= sprintf('</tr></table>');
}

else {
$navigation = "";
}

return $navigation;
}

?>
```

The Output

User Name
Username1
Username2
Username3
Username4
Username5
...
etc.

MySQLi Procedural

```php
<?php
session_start();

date_default_timezone_set("America/New_York");

error_reporting(E_ALL);
ini_set('display_errors', '1');

require( 'database.php' );

if (!isset($_SESSION['loggedin'])) {
    die("Not logged in");
//this causes to script to stop executing and lets the user
know there is a problem

/*
Note: instead of the die() function, you could use the
echo() function and provide an HTML link back to the login
page, or use the header() function to just redirect users
to the login page without any message. It is up to you to
decide how your application should function.
*/
}

elseif (isset($_SESSION['loggedin']) ){  //logged in

/* what a user would be able to do if logged in. It is up
to you to decide how your application should function. */

echo "Logged in as: {$_SESSION['loggedinuser']} ";
if ($_SESSION['adminuser']=='1'){ echo "- [ADMIN]";}
echo "<br/><br/>";

//Set this to the number of records per page
$limit = 5;
```

```php
for ($i=1; $i <= $pages; $i++) {   // loop thru
$newoffset=$limit*($i-1);
if ($newoffset != $offset) {
$navigation .= sprintf('<td><a
href="%s?offset=%s">%s</a></td>%s',
$_SERVER['PHP_SELF'], $newoffset, $i, "\n");
}
else {
$navigation .= sprintf('<td>%s</td>%s', $i, "\n");
}
}

//print next
$noffset = $pages*$limit-$limit;
if ($offset != $noffset)
{
$boffset = $offset+$limit;
$navigation .= sprintf('<td><a
href="%s?offset=%s">>></a></td>',
$_SERVER['PHP_SELF'], $boffset);
}

$navigation .= sprintf('</tr></table>');
}

else {
$navigation = "";
}

return $navigation;
}

?>
```

OUTPUT

Logged in as: bluebell

There are currently **14** Users.

Username

admin

admin2

bazc34

bluebell

carol45

Record(s) 1 - 5 of 14 | Page 1 2 3 >>

Back to Main page

Logout

MySQLi Object Oriented

```php
<?php
session_start();

date_default_timezone_set("America/New_York");

error_reporting(E_ALL);
ini_set('display_errors', '1');

require( 'database.php' );

if (!isset($_SESSION['loggedin'])) {
   die("Not logged in"); //this causes the script to stop
executing and lets the user know there is a problem

/*
Note: instead of the die() function, you could use the
echo() function and provide an HTML link back to the login
page, or use the header() function to just redirect users
to the login page without any message. It is up to you to
decide how your application should function.
*/
}

//else {   //logged in
elseif (isset($_SESSION['loggedin']) ){   //logged in

/* what a user would be able to do if logged in. It is up
to you to decide how your application should function. */

echo "Logged in as: {$_SESSION['loggedinuser']} ";
if ($_SESSION['adminuser']=='1'){ echo "- [ADMIN]";
      }
echo "<br/><br/>";

//setup variables
```

```php
//Set this to the number of records per page
$limit = 5;

if(isset($_GET['offset'])){
$offset=$_GET['offset'];
}
else{
//Set the initial offset
if (!isset($offset)) $offset = 0;
}

$offset = mysqli_real_escape_string($con, $offset);
$limit = mysqli_real_escape_string($con, $limit);

$result = $con->query("SELECT * FROM user ORDER BY username
LIMIT $offset, $limit");
$result_total = $con->query("SELECT * FROM user");
$totalcount = $result_total->num_rows;

echo "<br/>";
print("There are currently <b>$totalcount</b> Users.");
print("<br/><br/>\n");

echo "<table border='0'><tr>
<th>Username</th>
</tr>";

//$result->fetch_array(MYSQLI_BOTH); is the default
while($row = $result->fetch_array()){
echo "<tr>";
printf ("<td><a href=\"profile.php?uid=%s\">%s</a></td>",
$row['id'], $row['username']);
echo "</tr>";
}
echo "</table><br/>";

//print the links created by the navigation function
print get_nav($offset, $limit, $totalcount);
```

```php
echo "<p><a href=\"main.php\">Back to Main page</a></p>";
echo "<p><a href=\"logout.php\">Logout</a></p>";


}


function get_nav($offset, $limit, $totalnum) {
$navigation ='';

/* based the limit set for the number of records to show,
and the total number of records found, this function
calculates how many next, previous and page links to create
for navigation */

if ($totalnum > $limit) {
$navigation .= sprintf('<table><tr><td>');

// Print Record # - # of # (Customize to your need here)
$navigation   .= sprintf('Record(s) %s', ( $offset + 1 ));
$navigation   .= sprintf(' - ');
if( $offset + $limit >= $totalnum ){
$navigation   .= sprintf($totalnum);
}else{ $navigation   .= sprintf ( $offset + $limit ); }
$navigation   .= sprintf(' of %s     |    </td>', $totalnum);

$navigation .= sprintf('<td>Page </td>',"\n");

//print previous
if ($offset != 0) {
$boffset = $offset-$limit;
$navigation .= sprintf('<td><a
href="%s?offset=%s"><<</a></td>',$_SERVER['PHP_SELF'],$boff
set);
}

// calculate number of pages needing links
$pages = intval($totalnum/$limit);

// $pages now contains int of pages needed unless there is
a remainder from division
```

```php
if ($totalnum%$limit) $pages++;

//print pages
for ($i=1; $i <= $pages; $i++) {   // loop thru
$newoffset=$limit*($i-1);
if ($newoffset != $offset) {
$navigation .= sprintf('<td><a
href="%s?offset=%s">%s</a></td>%s',
$_SERVER['PHP_SELF'], $newoffset, $i, "\n");
}
else {
$navigation .= sprintf('<td>%s</td>%s', $i, "\n");
}
}

//print next
$noffset = $pages*$limit-$limit;
if ($offset != $noffset)
{
$boffset = $offset+$limit;
$navigation .= sprintf('<td><a
href="%s?offset=%s">>></a></td>',
$_SERVER['PHP_SELF'], $boffset);
}

$navigation .= sprintf('</tr></table>');
}

else {
$navigation = "";
}

return $navigation;
}

?>
```

PHP Data Object

```php
<?php
session_start();

date_default_timezone_set("America/New_York");

error_reporting(E_ALL);
ini_set('display_errors', '1');

require( 'database.php' );

if (!isset($_SESSION['loggedin'])) {
   die("Not logged in"); //this causes the script to stop
executing and lets the user know there is a problem

/*
Note: Instead of the die() function, you could use the
echo() function and provide an HTML link back to the login
page, or use the header() function to just redirect users
to the login page without any message. It is up to you to
decide how your application should behave.
*/
}

elseif (isset($_SESSION['loggedin']) ){  //logged in

/* what a user would be able to do if logged in. It is up
to you to decide how your application should behave. */

echo "Logged in as: {$_SESSION['loggedinuser']} ";
if ($_SESSION['adminuser']=='1'){ echo "- [ADMIN]";}
echo "<br/><br/>";

$totalquery = $con->query("SELECT count(id) FROM user");
$rows = $totalquery->fetchColumn();

$totalcount = $rows;
```

```php
//Set this to the number of records per page
$limit = 5;

if(isset($_GET['offset'])){
$offset=$_GET['offset'];
}
else{
//Set the initial offset
if (!isset($offset)) $offset = 0;
}

// make sure the variables are set to the type PDO is
expecting when you bind the parameters
$offset = (int)$offset;
$limit = (int)$limit;

//echo '<br/>offset: '.$offset.'<br/>';
//echo '<br/>limit: '.$limit.'<br/>';

/*** prepare the SQL statement ***/
$result_all = $con->prepare("SELECT * FROM user order by
username LIMIT ?, ?");

/*** bind the parameters ***/
$result_all->bindParam(1, $offset, PDO::PARAM_INT);
$result_all->bindParam(2, $limit, PDO::PARAM_INT);

/*** execute the prepared statement ***/
$result_all->execute();

/* Bind by column number */
$result_all->bindColumn(1, $id);
$result_all->bindColumn(2, $username);

echo "<br/>";
print("There are currently <b>$totalcount</b> Users.");
print("<br/><br/>\n");
```

```php
echo "<table border='0'><tr>
<th>Username</th>
</tr>";

while ($result_all->fetch()) {
echo "<tr>";
printf ("<td><a href=\"profile.php?uid=%s\">%s</a></td>",
$id, $username);
echo "</tr>";
}
echo "</table><br/>";

//print the links created by the navigation function
print get_nav($offset, $limit, $totalcount);

echo "<p><a href=\"main.php\">Back to Main page</a></p>";
echo "<p><a href=\"logout.php\">Logout</a></p>";

}

function get_nav($offset, $limit, $totalnum) {
$navigation ='';

/* based the limit set for the number of records to show,
and the total number of records found, this function
calculates how many next, previous and page links to create
for navigation */

if ($totalnum > $limit) {
$navigation .= sprintf('<table><tr><td>');
// Print Record # - # of # (Customize to your need here)
$navigation  .= sprintf('Record(s) %s', ( $offset + 1 ));
$navigation  .= sprintf(' - ');
if( $offset + $limit >= $totalnum ){
$navigation  .= sprintf($totalnum);
}else{ $navigation  .= sprintf ( $offset + $limit ); }
$navigation  .= sprintf(' of %s    |    </td>', $totalnum);

$navigation .= sprintf('<td>Page </td>',"\n");
```

```php
//print previous
if ($offset != 0) {
$boffset = $offset-$limit;
$navigation .= sprintf('<td><a
href="%s?offset=%s"><<<</a></td>',$_SERVER['PHP_SELF'],$boff
set);
}

// calculate number of pages needing links
$pages = intval($totalnum/$limit);

// $pages now contains int of pages needed unless there is
a remainder from division
if ($totalnum%$limit) $pages++;

//print pages
for ($i=1; $i <= $pages; $i++) {   // loop thru
$newoffset=$limit*($i-1);
if ($newoffset != $offset) {
$navigation .= sprintf('<td><a
href="%s?offset=%s">%s</a></td>%s',
$_SERVER['PHP_SELF'], $newoffset, $i, "\n");
}
else {
$navigation .= sprintf('<td>%s</td>%s', $i, "\n");
}
}

//print next
$noffset = $pages*$limit-$limit;
if ($offset != $noffset)
{
$boffset = $offset+$limit;
$navigation .= sprintf('<td><a
href="%s?offset=%s">>></a></td>',
$_SERVER['PHP_SELF'], $boffset);
}
```

```php
$navigation .= sprintf('</tr></table>');
}

else {
$navigation = "";
}

return $navigation;
}

?>
```

4.2 Step 2: Viewing the User Profile

The profile page script – displays information about individual users of the website.

This particular script will show the username and email for the specific user selected from the membership list. A profile page can display a wide variety of information limited by what data the user table (and perhaps other tables) collects and what information the profile page is coded to make public. In some membership applications, the user also has the ability to determine how much or how little of their information will be public, and appear on their profile page.

Note: You would probably not show the user's email on their profile page usually. If your user table records the date the user created the account and when they last logged in, then the profile script can display this information instead.

"profile.php"

CODE

MySQL

```php
<?php
session_start();

date_default_timezone_set("America/New_York");

error_reporting(E_ALL);
ini_set('display_errors', '1');

require( 'database.php' );

if (!$_SESSION['loggedin']) {
die("Not logged in");
```

```php
//this causes the script to stop executing and lets the
user know there is a problem

/* Note: Instead of the die() function, you could use the
echo() function and provide an HTML link back to the login
page, or use the header() function to just redirect users
to the login page without any message. It is up to you to
decide how your application should function.
*/

}
else {

//else {   //logged in
elseif (isset($_SESSION['loggedin']) ){   //logged in

/* what a user would be able to do if logged in. It is up
to you to decide how your application should function. */

echo "Logged in as: {$_SESSION['loggedinuser']} ";
if ($_SESSION['adminuser']=='1'){ echo "- [ADMIN]";}
echo "<br/><br/>";

if(isset($_GET['uid'])){

$uid=$_GET['uid'];

// query the DB
$sql = "SELECT * FROM user WHERE id=$uid";
$result = mysql_query($sql);
$myrow = mysql_fetch_array($result);
?>

<p>
<b>
<font color="#9c2108">member:
<? echo $myrow["username"]; ?>
</font>
</b>
```

```
</p>

<br/>
<table border="0" cellpadding="1" cellspacing="0"
width="500">
<tr>
<td align=left width=150>Username :</td>
<td align=left width=350><?php echo $myrow["username"] ?>
</td>
</tr>
<tr>
 <td align=left>Email Address :</td>
<td align=left><?php echo $myrow["email"]; ?></td></tr>
</table>
</table>

<?php

} else {

?>

<p>
<b>
<font color="#9c2108">No user selected.</font>
</b>
</p>

<?php
}

if (!$referer == '') {
 echo '<p><a href="' . $referer . '" title="Return to the
previous page">&laquo; Go back</a></p>';
} else {
echo '<p><a href="javascript:history.go(-1)" title="Return
to the previous page">&laquo; back to members list
</a></p>';
}
```

```
echo "<p><a href=\"protected_page.php\">Back to Main
page</a></p>";
echo "<p><a href=\"logout.php\">Logout</a></p>";
}
?>
```

MySQLi Procedural

```php
<?php
session_start();

date_default_timezone_set("America/New_York");

error_reporting(E_ALL);
ini_set('display_errors', '1');

require( 'database.php' );

if (!isset($_SESSION['loggedin'])) {
   die("Not logged in"); //this causes the script to stop
executing and lets the user know there is a problem

/*
Note: Instead of the die() function, you could use the
echo() function and provide an HTML link back to the login
page, or use the header() function to just redirect users
to the login page without any message. It is up to you to
decide what your application should function.
*/

}

//else {   //logged in
elseif (isset($_SESSION['loggedin']) ){   //logged in

/* what a user would be able to do if logged in. It is up
to you to decide how your application should function. */

echo "Logged in as: {$_SESSION['loggedinuser']} ";
if ($_SESSION['adminuser']=='1'){ echo "- [ADMIN]";}
echo "<br/><br/>";

if(isset($_GET['uid'])){
```

```php
$uid = mysqli_real_escape_string($con, $_GET['uid']);

// query the DB
$sql = "SELECT * FROM user WHERE id=$uid";
$result = mysqli_query($con, $sql);

$myrow = mysqli_fetch_array($result);

?>

<p>
<b>
<font color="#9c2108">member: <? echo $myrow["username"];
?></font>
</b>
</p>

<table border="0" cellpadding="1" cellspacing="0"
width="500">
<tr>
<td align=left width=150>Username :</td>
<td align=left width=350><?php echo $myrow["username"] ?>
</td>
</tr>
<tr>
 <td align=left>Email Address :</td>
<td align=left><?php echo $myrow["email"]; ?></td></tr>
</table>

<?php

} else {

?>

<p>
<b>
<font color="#9c2108">No user selected.</font>
</b>
```

```
</p>

<?php
}

if(isset($_GET['referer'])) {
  $referer = trim($_POST['referer']);
} elseif (isset($_SERVER['HTTP_REFERER'])) {
  $referer = $_SERVER['HTTP_REFERER'];
} else {
  $referer = "";
}

if (!$referer == '') {
 echo '<p><a href="' . $referer . '" title="Return to the
previous page">&laquo; Go back</a></p>';
} else {
echo '<p><a href="javascript:history.go(-1)" title="Return
to the previous page">&laquo; back to members list
</a></p>';
}
echo "<p><a href=\"main.php\">Back to Main page</a></p>";
echo "<p><a href=\"logout.php\">Logout</a></p>";
}

?>
```

MySQLi Object Oriented

```php
<?php
session_start();

date_default_timezone_set("America/New_York");

error_reporting(E_ALL);
ini_set('display_errors', '1');

require( 'database.php' );

if (!isset($_SESSION['loggedin'])) {
   die("Not logged in"); //this causes the script to stop
executing and lets the user know there is a problem

/*
Note: Instead of the die() function, you could use the
echo() function and provide an HTML link back to the login
page, or use the header() function to just redirect users
to the login page without any message. It is up to you to
decide what your application should function.
*/

}

//else {  //logged in
elseif (isset($_SESSION['loggedin']) ){  //logged in

/* what a user would be able to do if logged in. It is up
to you to decide how your application should function. */

echo "Logged in as: {$_SESSION['loggedinuser']} ";
if ($_SESSION['adminuser']=='1'){ echo "- [ADMIN]";}
echo "<br/><br/>";

if(isset($_GET['uid'])){
$uid = mysqli_real_escape_string($con, $_GET['uid']);
```

```php
// query the DB
$sql = "SELECT * FROM user WHERE id=$uid";
$result = $con->query($sql);

$myrow = $result->fetch_array();

?>

<p>
<b>
<font color="#9c2108">member: <? echo $myrow["username"];
?></font>
</b>
</p>

<table border="0" cellpadding="1" cellspacing="0"
width="500">
<tr>
<td align=left width=150>Username :</td>
<td align=left width=350><?php echo $myrow["username"] ?>
</td>
</tr>
<tr>
 <td align=left>Email Address :</td>
<td align=left><?php echo $myrow["email"]; ?></td></tr>
</table>

<?php

} else {

?>

<p>
<b>
<font color="#9c2108">No user selected.</font>
</b>
</p>
```

```php
<?php
}

if(isset($_GET['referer'])) {
  $referer = trim($_POST['referer']);
} elseif (isset($_SERVER['HTTP_REFERER'])) {
  $referer = $_SERVER['HTTP_REFERER'];
} else {
  $referer = "";
}

if (!$referer == '') {
 echo '<p><a href="' . $referer . '" title="Return to the
previous page">&laquo; Go back</a></p>';
} else {
echo '<p><a href="javascript:history.go(-1)" title="Return
to the previous page">&laquo; back to members list
</a></p>';
}
echo "<p><a href=\"main.php\">Back to Main page</a></p>";
echo "<p><a href=\"logout.php\">Logout</a></p>";
}

?>
```

PHP Data Object

```php
<?php
session_start();

date_default_timezone_set("America/New_York");

error_reporting(E_ALL);
ini_set('display_errors', '1');

require( 'database.php' );

if (!isset($_SESSION['loggedin'])) {
   die("Not logged in"); //this causes the script to stop
executing and lets the user know there is a problem

/*
Note:  instead of the die() function, you could use the
echo() function and provide an HTML link back to the login
page, or use the header() function to just redirect users
to the login page without any message. It is up to you to
decide what your application should behave.
*/
}

elseif (isset($_SESSION['loggedin']) ){  //logged in

/* what a user would be able to do if logged in. It is up
to you to decide how your application should behave. */

echo "Logged in as: {$_SESSION['loggedinuser']} ";
if ($_SESSION['adminuser']=='1'){ echo "- [ADMIN]";}
echo "<br/><br/>";


if(isset($_GET['uid'])){
$uid = $_GET['uid'];
```

```php
// display the user profile

    // query the DB

    $sql = "SELECT * FROM user WHERE id = ?";

    try{
    $result = $con->prepare($sql);
    $result->bindParam(1, $uid, PDO::PARAM_INT);
     $result->execute();

    /* bind result variables */
    //$result->bindColumn(1, $id);
    //bind additional results if needed
    $result->bindColumn(2, $username);
    //$result->bindColumn(3, $password);
    $result->bindColumn(4, $email);
    //$result->bindColumn(5, $level);
            }
    catch (PDOException $e)
    {
     $error = 'Error: ' . $e->getMessage();
         echo $error;
         //exit();
    }

         $result->fetch();
?>

<p>
<b>
<font color="#9c2108">member: <? echo $username; ?></font>
</b>
</p>

<table border="0" cellpadding="1" cellspacing="0"
width="500">
<tr>
<td align=left width=150>Username :</td>
```

```php
<td align=left width=350><?php echo $username; ?> </td>
</tr>
<tr>
 <td align=left>Email Address :</td>
<td align=left><?php echo $email; ?></td></tr>
</table>

<?php

} else {

?>

<p>
<b>
<font color="#9c2108">No user selected.</font>
</b>
</p>

<?php
}

if(isset($_GET['referer'])) {
  $referer = trim($_POST['referer']);
} elseif (isset($_SERVER['HTTP_REFERER'])) {
  $referer = $_SERVER['HTTP_REFERER'];
} else {
  $referer = "";
}

if (!$referer == '') {
 echo '<p><a href="' . $referer . '" title="Return to the
previous page">&laquo; Go back</a></p>';
} else {
echo '<p><a href="javascript:history.go(-1)" title="Return
to the previous page">&laquo; back to members list
</a></p>';
}
echo "<p><a href=\"main.php\">Back to Main page</a></p>";
```

```
echo "<p><a href=\"logout.php\">Logout</a></p>";
}
?>
```

5. Building the Member/User Administration Backend of your Website

The administrator of your website needs to be able to do several keys things to manage the users of your website: find a user, update/change user information and delete a user. The admin backend can be coded as several separate scripts or as one script. The admin backend for this particular membership application is coded to accomplish all three key functions in one script. The admin script will be explained in sections because the complete script is several hundred lines long.

Two views:

a) List the total number of users on the main admin page with the option to find users by letters of the alphabet or view all users.

b) Show individual user profiles with the option to edit user information or delete the user.

The admin script first gets the total number of users and stores it into a variable, then uses that information along with the values of other variables (whether passed via the GET or POST methods) to control the execution of code. The overall logic of the script is outlined below:

"admin.php"

CODE

```php
<?php
// count users
...

//sets the values for the variables regardless of GET/POST
method
...
```

```php
// search for users by the first letter in username
if ($let):

// if passed searchwords
elseif ($finduser):
...

// if passed the userid, take one of several actions:
delete/update/display user profile
elseif ($uid):
...

// show a list of all users
elseif($viewall):
...

// main page of user admin application
else:
...

endif;

function get_nav($offset, $limit, $totalnum, $type =
"normal") {
...

}
?>
```

5.1 Step 1: The Main Page

The first page an administrator sees, once the admin script is accessed will have the alphabet displayed in a table of multiple rows, and a button to click on to view all users.

OUTPUT

Logged in as: admin - [ADMIN]

There are currently **14** Users.

Search by letter

A B C D E
F G H I J
K L M N O
P Q R S T
U V W X Y
Z

Search for: [   ]
[Find User]

Or View all Users
[Viewall]

Logout

Generating the table

Generate a table of letters from A to Z with links. Using a combination of the chr() function, for-loops and the PHP modulus operator (%), this table can be created automatically. Each row in the table has five letters – five columns with one letter in each column. To change the number of columns in each row, change the divider in the if() conditional statement e.g. ($i % 10) will generate a table of three rows (two rows of ten letters and one of six letters).

The numbers used in the for-loop for the letter variable are significant. They correspond to the ascii character codes for uppercase A-Z. When the links are generated, I also add 32 to the letter variable because the new number, after the addition, corresponds to the ascii character codes for lowercase a-z. The links will appear as uppercase letters but the letter variable being passed into the script is lowercase.

CODE

```
// main page of user admin application

} else {

print "";
print("There are currently <b>$total</b> Users.");
print("<br/><br/>\n");
print "Search by letter<p>";

for ($i = 65 ; $i < 91 ; $i++){

// if $i is non-zero and is divisible by 5 print a line
break.
//# Create a new row every five columns
if (($i % 5 == 0) && ($i!=0)){
 echo "<br />";
}
```

```php
//# Add a column
printf ('<a href = "%s?let=%s">%s</a> ',
$_SERVER['PHP_SELF'], chr($i+32), chr($i));
}

?>
<br/><br/>
<form method="post" action="<?php echo
$_SERVER['SCRIPT_NAME']; ?>">
Search for: <input type="text" name="searchwords"
value=""><br>
<input type="submit" name="finduser" value="Find User">
</form>

<br/><br/> Or View all Users
<form method="post" action="<?php echo
$_SERVER['SCRIPT_NAME']; ?>">
<input type=submit name="viewall" value="Viewall">
</form>

<?php
}
?>
</td></tr>
</table>

<?php

echo "<p><a href=\"logout.php\">Logout</a></p>";
}
```

5.2 Step 2: Viewing all Users

The more members your site gains, the longer your membership list. The limit and offset variables are used to limit the number of total results viewed at one time. They are also used for pagination – creating the page links for the username results.

CODE

MySQL

```
// show a list of all users

elseif ($viewall):

// display list of users
$result_all = mysql_query ("SELECT id, username FROM user
order by username LIMIT $offset, $limit");

print ("There are currently <b>$total</b> Users.");
print ("<br/><br/>\n");

while ($myrow = mysql_fetch_array ($result_all)) {
printf ("<a href=\"%s?uid=%s\">%s</a><br/>\n",
$_SERVER['PHP_SELF'],
$myrow["id"], $myrow["username"]);
}

print "<br/>". get_nav ($offset, $limit, $total);

?>
</td></tr>

<tr><td><br/>
<a href="<?php echo
$_SERVER['PHP_SELF']."?viewall=viewall"; ?>">View list</a>
```

```
</td></tr>

<tr><td>
<a href="<?php echo $_SERVER['PHP_SELF']; ?>">Main Menu</a>
```

OUTPUT

Logged in as: admin - [ADMIN]

There are currently **14** Users.

admin
admin2
bazc34
bluebell
carol45

Record(s) 1 - 5 of 14 | Page 1 2 3 >>

View list

Main Menu

Logout

Logged in as: admin - [ADMIN]

There are currently **14** Users.

fifa
johndoe
lifesaver
penny
summer23

Record(s) 6 - 10 of 14 | Page << 1 2 3 >>

View list

Main Menu

Logout

MySQLi Procedural

```
// show a list of all users

} elseif ($viewall){

 // display list of users
$result_all = mysqli_query($con, "SELECT id,username FROM
user order by username LIMIT $offset, $limit");

print("There are currently <b>$total</b> Users.");
print("<br/><br/>\n");

while ($myrow = mysqli_fetch_array($result_all)) {
printf("<a href=\"%s?uid=%s\">%s</a><br/>\n",
$_SERVER['PHP_SELF'],
$myrow["id"], $myrow["username"]);
}...
```

MySQLi Object-Oriented

```
// show a list of all users
} elseif($viewall){

 // display list of users
$result_all = $con->query("SELECT id,username FROM user
order by username LIMIT $offset, $limit");

print("There are currently <b>$total</b> Users.");
print("<br/><br/>\n");

while ($myrow = $result_all->fetch_array()) {
printf("<a href=\"%s?uid=%s\">%s</a><br/>\n",
$_SERVER['PHP_SELF'],
$myrow["id"], $myrow["username"]);
}
...
```

PHP Data Object

```php
// show a list of all users

} elseif($viewall){
 // display list of users

// make sure the variables are set to the type PDO is
expecting when you bind the parameters
$offset = (int)$offset;
$limit = (int)$limit;

try{

/*** prepare the SQL statement ***/
$result_all = $con->prepare("SELECT id,username FROM user
order by username LIMIT ?, ?");

/*** bind the parameters ***/
$result_all->bindParam(1, $offset, PDO::PARAM_INT);
$result_all->bindParam(2, $limit, PDO::PARAM_INT);

/*** execute the prepared statement ***/
$result_all->execute();

/* Bind by column number */
$result_all->bindColumn(1, $id);
$result_all->bindColumn(2, $username);
}
 catch (PDOException $e)
{
    $error = 'Error: ' . $e->getMessage();
    echo $error;
    //exit();
}

print("There are currently <b>$total</b> Users.");
print("<br/><br/>\n");
```

```
while ($result_all->fetch()) {
printf("<a href=\"%s?uid=%s\">%s</a><br/>\n",
$_SERVER['PHP_SELF'],
$id, $username);
}
...
```

5.3 Step 3: View all Users by First Letter Matching

If you do not want to navigate through the list of usernames and you know the starting character/letter of the username you are looking for, you can search by letter. Clicking on a letter link in the table, passes the letter variable into the admin script, for use in an SQL statement that selects records containing a username that starts with the letter. Pagination is again used to break the results into manageable chunks.

CODE

MySQL

```
// search for users by the first letter in username
if ($let):

$letter_total= mysql_query("select id,username from user
where username like '$let%'");
$numrows_letter= mysql_num_rows($letter_total);

$letter= mysql_query("select id,username from user where
username like '$let%'
        LIMIT $offset, $limit");

  if (mysql_num_rows($letter)>0) {
        $numrows= mysql_num_rows($letter);
        $x=0;
        while ($x<$numrows){
        $id= mysql_result($letter,$x, id);
 $username= mysql_result($letter,$x, username);
printf("<a href=\"%s?uid=%s\">%s</a><br/>\n",
$_SERVER['PHP_SELF'],$id, $username);
        $x++;

        }
```

```php
print "<br/>". get_nav($offset, $limit,
$numrows_letter,"letter");

?>
</td></tr>
<tr><td>
<a href="<?php echo
$_SERVER['PHP_SELF']."?viewall=viewall"; ?>">View list</a>
</td></tr>
<tr><td>
<a href="<?php echo $_SERVER['PHP_SELF']; ?>">Main Menu</a>
<?
 }
else{
print "<tr><td align=left colSpan=3 valign=top width=500>
    No records found for letter <b>$let</b></td></tr>";
?>
<tr><td><br/>
<a href="<?php echo
$_SERVER['PHP_SELF']."?viewall=viewall"; ?>">View list</a>
</td></tr>
<tr><td>
<a href="<?php echo $_SERVER['PHP_SELF']; ?>">Main Menu</a>
<?
   }
```

MySQLi Procedural

```
// search for users by the first letter in username

if ($let){

$letter_total= mysqli_query($con, "select id,username from
user where username like '$let%'");
$numrows_letter= mysqli_num_rows($letter_total);

$letter= mysqli_query($con, "select id,username from user
where username like '$let%'
        LIMIT $offset, $limit");

//there is no equivalent in MySQLi to the mysql_result
function
//you can use the mysqli_fetch() functions instead

if (mysqli_num_rows($letter)>0) {

 /* Get field information for all fields */
    //while ($row = mysqli_fetch_row($letter)) {
        while ($row = mysqli_fetch_array($letter)) {

    //printf("<a href=\"%s?uid=%s\">%s</a><br/>\n",
$_SERVER['PHP_SELF'],$row[0], $row[1]);
        printf("<a href=\"%s?uid=%s\">%s</a><br/>\n",
$_SERVER['PHP_SELF'],$row["id"], $row["username"]);
    }
    mysqli_free_result($letter);

printf("<a href=\"%s?uid=%s\">%s</a><br/>\n",
$_SERVER['PHP_SELF'],$id, $username);

 $x++;

 }
```

```php
print "<br/>". get_nav($offset, $limit,
$numrows_letter,"letter");

?>
</td></tr>
<tr><td>
<a href="<?php echo
$_SERVER['PHP_SELF']."?viewall=viewall"; ?>">View list</a>
</td></tr>
<tr><td>
<a href="<?php echo $_SERVER['PHP_SELF']; ?>">Main Menu</a>
<?php
    }
else{
print "<tr><td align=left colSpan=3 valign=top width=500>
    No records found for letter <b>$let</b></td></tr>";
?>
<tr><td><br/>
<a href="<?php echo
$_SERVER['PHP_SELF']."?viewall=viewall"; ?>">View list</a>
</td></tr>
<tr><td>
<a href="<?php echo $_SERVER['PHP_SELF']; ?>">Main Menu</a>

<?php

    }
```

You can also create a custom function that duplicates the functionality of the original MySQL result function, include it in your script and call that function wherever you made calls to mysql_result().

```php
// search for users by the first letter in username

if ($let){

$letter_total= mysqli_query($con, "select id,username from
user where username like '$let%'");
```

```php
$numrows_letter= mysqli_num_rows($letter_total);

$letter= mysqli_query($con, "select id,username from user
where username like '$let%'
        LIMIT $offset, $limit");

//there is no equivalent in MySQLi to the mysql_result
function
//you can create a custom function that replicates the
functionality

function mysqli_result($result, $iRow = 0, $sField = '')
{
    $return = false;
    if (mysqli_data_seek($result, $iRow))
    {
        $record = mysqli_fetch_array($result);
        if (empty($sField) && isset($record[0]))
        {
            $return = $record[0];
        }
        elseif (!empty($sField) && isset($record[$sField]))
        {
            $return = $record[$sField];
        }
    }
    return $return;
}

 if (mysqli_num_rows($letter)>0) {

$numrows= mysqli_num_rows($letter);

 $x=0;

 while ($x<$numrows){

 $id= mysqli_result($letter,$x, 'id');
 $username= mysqli_result($letter,$x, 'username');
```

```php
printf("<a href=\"%s?uid=%s\">%s</a><br/>\n",
$_SERVER['PHP_SELF'],$id, $username);

  $x++;

  }

print "<br/>". get_nav($offset, $limit,
$numrows_letter,"letter");

?>
</td></tr>
<tr><td>
<a href="<?php echo
$_SERVER['PHP_SELF']."?viewall=viewall"; ?>">View list</a>
</td></tr>
<tr><td>
<a href="<?php echo $_SERVER['PHP_SELF']; ?>">Main Menu</a>
<?php
  }
else{
print "<tr><td align=left colSpan=3 valign=top width=500>
    No records found for letter <b>$let</b></td></tr>";
?>
<tr><td><br/>
<a href="<?php echo
$_SERVER['PHP_SELF']."?viewall=viewall"; ?>">View list</a>
</td></tr>
<tr><td>
<a href="<?php echo $_SERVER['PHP_SELF']; ?>">Main Menu</a>

<?php

  }
```

MySQLi Object-Oriented

```
// search for users by the first letter in username

if ($let){

$letter_total= mysqli_query($con, "select id,username from
user where username like '$let%'");
$numrows_letter= mysqli_num_rows($letter_total);

$letter= mysqli_query($con, "select id,username from user
where username like '$let%'
        LIMIT $offset, $limit");

//there is no equivalent in MySQLi to the mysql_result
function
//you can use the mysqli_fetch() functions instead

if (mysqli_num_rows($letter)>0) {

 /* Get field information for all fields */
    //while ($row = mysqli_fetch_row($letter)) {
        while ($row = mysqli_fetch_array($letter)) {

    //printf("<a href=\"%s?uid=%s\">%s</a><br/>\n",
$_SERVER['PHP_SELF'],$row[0], $row[1]);
        printf("<a href=\"%s?uid=%s\">%s</a><br/>\n",
$_SERVER['PHP_SELF'],$row["id"], $row["username"]);
    }
    mysqli_free_result($letter);

printf("<a href=\"%s?uid=%s\">%s</a><br/>\n",
$_SERVER['PHP_SELF'],$id, $username);

 $x++;

 }
```

```php
print "<br/>". get_nav($offset, $limit,
$numrows_letter,"letter");

?>
</td></tr>
<tr><td>
<a href="<?php echo
$_SERVER['PHP_SELF']."?viewall=viewall"; ?>">View list</a>
</td></tr>
<tr><td>
<a href="<?php echo $_SERVER['PHP_SELF']; ?>">Main Menu</a>
<?php
 }
else{
print "<tr><td align=left colSpan=3 valign=top width=500>
    No records found for letter <b>$let</b></td></tr>";
?>
<tr><td><br/>
<a href="<?php echo
$_SERVER['PHP_SELF']."?viewall=viewall"; ?>">View list</a>
</td></tr>
<tr><td>
<a href="<?php echo $_SERVER['PHP_SELF']; ?>">Main Menu</a>

<?php

    }
```

You can also create a custom function that duplicates the functionality of the original MySQL result function, include it in your script and call that function wherever you made calls to mysql_result().

```php
// search for users by the first letter in username

if ($let){

$letter_total= mysqli_query($con, "select id,username from
user where username like '$let%'");
```

```php
$numrows_letter= mysqli_num_rows($letter_total);

$letter= mysqli_query($con, "select id,username from user
where username like '$let%'
        LIMIT $offset, $limit");

//there is no equivalent in MySQLi to the mysql_result
function
//you can create a custom function that replicates the
functionality

function mysqli_result($result, $iRow = 0, $sField = '')
{
    $return = false;
    if (mysqli_data_seek($result, $iRow))
    {
        $record = mysqli_fetch_array($result);
        if (empty($sField) && isset($record[0]))
        {
            $return = $record[0];
        }
        elseif (!empty($sField) && isset($record[$sField]))
        {
            $return = $record[$sField];
        }
    }
    return $return;
}

 if (mysqli_num_rows($letter)>0) {

$numrows= mysqli_num_rows($letter);

 $x=0;

 while ($x<$numrows){

 $id= mysqli_result($letter,$x, 'id');
 $username= mysqli_result($letter,$x, 'username');
```

```php
printf("<a href=\"%s?uid=%s\">%s</a><br/>\n",
$_SERVER['PHP_SELF'],$id, $username);

$x++;

}

print "<br/>". get_nav($offset, $limit,
$numrows_letter,"letter");

?>
</td></tr>
<tr><td>
<a href="<?php echo
$_SERVER['PHP_SELF']."?viewall=viewall"; ?>">View list</a>
</td></tr>
<tr><td>
<a href="<?php echo $_SERVER['PHP_SELF']; ?>">Main Menu</a>
<?php
}
else{
print "<tr><td align=left colSpan=3 valign=top width=500>
No records found for letter <b>$let</b></td></tr>";
?>
<tr><td><br/>
<a href="<?php echo
$_SERVER['PHP_SELF']."?viewall=viewall"; ?>">View list</a>
</td></tr>
<tr><td>
<a href="<?php echo $_SERVER['PHP_SELF']; ?>">Main Menu</a>

<?php

}
```

PHP Data Object

```php
// search for users by the first letter in username

if ($let){

try{
$letter_total= $con->prepare("select count(*) from (select
distinct id,username from user where username like
CONCAT(?, '%')) u");

$letter_total->bindParam('1', $let, PDO::PARAM_STR);
$letter_total->execute();

}
 catch (PDOException $e)
{
    $error = 'Error: ' . $e->getMessage();
    echo $error;
    //exit();
}

$numrows_letter = $letter_total->fetchColumn();
//echo $numrows_letter;

// Close the cursor
/* The following call to closeCursor() may be required by
some drivers */
$letter_total->closeCursor();

try{
$letter= $con->prepare("select id,username from user where
username like CONCAT(?, '%') LIMIT ?, ?");
//echo $con->error;
//$letter->bindParam('sdd', $let, $offset, $limit);
$letter->bindParam(1, $let, PDO::PARAM_STR);
$letter->bindParam(2, $offset, PDO::PARAM_INT);
$letter->bindParam(3, $limit, PDO::PARAM_INT);
```

```php
$letter->execute();

    // Bind by column number
    $letter->bindColumn(1, $id);
    $letter->bindColumn(2, $username);

    /*
    // Bind by column name
    $letter->bindColumn('id', $id);
    $letter->bindColumn('username', $username);

    // You can also specify a data type when binding
columns
    $letter->bindColumn('id', $id, PDO::PARAM_INT);
    $letter->bindColumn('username', $username,
PDO::PARAM_STR);
    */
}
 catch (PDOException $e)
{
    $error = 'Error: ' . $e->getMessage();
    echo $error;
    //exit();
}

 if ($numrows_letter > 0) {

 while ($letter->fetch()){

printf("<a href=\"%s?uid=%s\">%s</a><br/>\n",
$_SERVER['PHP_SELF'],$id, $username);

 }

// Close the cursor
/* The following call to closeCursor() may be required by
some drivers */
$letter->closeCursor();
```

```php
print "<br/>". get_nav($offset, $limit,
$numrows_letter,"letter");

?>
</td></tr>
<tr><td>
<a href="<?php echo
$_SERVER['PHP_SELF']."?viewall=viewall"; ?>">View list</a>
</td></tr>
<tr><td>
<a href="<?php echo $_SERVER['PHP_SELF']; ?>">Main Menu</a>
<?php
  }
else{
print "<tr><td align=left colSpan=3 valign=top width=500>
    No records found for letter <b>$let</b></td></tr>";
?>
<tr><td><br/>
<a href="<?php echo
$_SERVER['PHP_SELF']."?viewall=viewall"; ?>">View list</a>
</td></tr>
<tr><td>
<a href="<?php echo $_SERVER['PHP_SELF']; ?>">Main Menu</a>
<?php

  }
```

5.4 Step 4: Find User with Username or Email Matching Search words

To find a specific user, you can collect 'search words' via a search form. Once the admin script receives the 'search words,' it will create SQL statements to search for a matching username or email address. The **$fieldstosearch** array defines which fields in the user table are used to create the SQL statements. A for loop creates a partial where clause string for each field in the array. The partial where clause is used in the full SQL statement.

Note: The substr() function is used to remove the extra 'OR' from the end of the partial where clause string, after the last field to search is added to the string.

CODE

MySQL

```
// if passed searchwords, try to find matching user(s)

} elseif ($finduser){
...
}
//print field(s) query, this is optional
print $clause."<p>";

$searchq = mysql_query("SELECT id from user WHERE
$clause");
$numrows_search = mysql_num_rows($searchq);

$realsql = "SELECT * from user WHERE $clause LIMIT $offset,
$limit";
$result = mysql_query($realsql);
if (mysql_num_rows($result) > 0) {
$itemnum=$offset+1;
while($row = mysql_fetch_array($result)) {
```

```php
printf("%s <a href=\"%s?uid=%s\">%s</a><br/>\n",
$itemnum++, $_SERVER['PHP_SELF'],
$row["id"], $row["username"]);
}
}
else {
print "Sorry No records found";
}

print "<br/>". get_nav($offset, $limit, $numrows_search,
"usersearch");

}
?>

<tr><td><br/>
<a href="<?php echo
$_SERVER['PHP_SELF']."?viewall=viewall"; ?>">View list</a>
</td></tr>
<tr><td>
<a href="<?php echo $_SERVER['PHP_SELF']; ?>">Main Menu</a>
```

MySQLi Procedural

```
// if passed searchwords, try to find matching user(s)

} elseif ($finduser){
…
}
//print field(s) query, this is optional
print $clause."<p>";

$searchq = mysqli_query($con, "SELECT id from user WHERE
$clause");
$numrows_search = mysqli_num_rows($searchq);

$realsql = "SELECT * from user WHERE $clause LIMIT $offset,
$limit";
$result = mysqli_query($con, $realsql);
if (mysqli_num_rows($result) > 0) {
$itemnum=$offset+1;
while($row = mysqli_fetch_array($result)) {
printf("%s <a href=\"%s?uid=%s\">%s</a><br/>\n",
$itemnum++, $_SERVER['PHP_SELF'],
$row["id"], $row["username"]);
}
}
else {
print "Sorry No records found";
}

print "<br/>". get_nav($offset, $limit, $numrows_search,
"usersearch");

}
?>

<tr><td><br/>
<a href="<?php echo
$_SERVER['PHP_SELF']."?viewall=viewall"; ?>">View list</a>
```

```
</td></tr>

<tr><td>
<a href="<?php echo $_SERVER['PHP_SELF']; ?>">Main Menu</a>
```

MySQLi Object-Oriented

```php
// if passed searchwords, try to find matching user(s)

} elseif ($finduser){
...
}
//print field(s) query, this is optional
print $clause."<p>";

$searchq = $con->query("SELECT id from user WHERE
$clause");
$numrows_search =$searchq->num_rows;

$realsql = "SELECT * from user WHERE $clause LIMIT $offset,
$limit";
$result = $con->query($realsql);
if ($result->num_rows > 0) {
$itemnum=$offset+1;
while($row = $result->fetch_array()) {
printf("%s <a href=\"%s?uid=%s\">%s</a><br/>\n",
$itemnum++, $_SERVER['PHP_SELF'],
$row["id"], $row["username"]);
}
}
else {
print "Sorry No records found";
}

print "<br/>". get_nav($offset, $limit, $numrows_search,
"usersearch");

}
?>
<tr><td><br/>
<a href="<?php echo
$_SERVER['PHP_SELF']."?viewall=viewall"; ?>">View list</a>
</td></tr>
```

```
<tr><td>
<a href="<?php echo $_SERVER['PHP_SELF']; ?>">Main Menu</a>
```

PHP Data Object

```php
// if passed searchwords, try to find matching user(s)

} elseif ($finduser){
…
}
//print field(s) in query, this is optional
print $clause."<p>";

try{
$searchq = $con->prepare("SELECT count(id) from user WHERE
$clause");
$searchq->execute();

}
catch (PDOException $e)
{
$error = 'Error: ' . $e->getMessage();
echo $error;
//exit();
}


$numrows_search = $searchq->fetchColumn();

try{
$result = $con->prepare("SELECT id, username from user
WHERE $clause LIMIT $offset, $limit");
$result->bindParam(1, $offset, PDO::PARAM_INT);
$result->bindParam(2, $limit, PDO::PARAM_INT);
$result->execute();

// Bind by column number
$result->bindColumn(1, $id);
$result->bindColumn(2, $username);
}
catch (PDOException $e)
{
```

```php
$error = 'Error: ' . $e->getMessage();
echo $error;
//exit();
}

if ($numrows_search > 0) {
$itemnum=$offset+1;

while($row = $result->fetch()) {
printf("%s <a href=\"%s?uid=%s\">%s</a><br/>\n",
$itemnum++, $_SERVER['PHP_SELF'], $id, $username);
}

}
else {
print "Sorry No records found";
}

print "<br/>". get_nav($offset, $limit, $numrows_search,
"usersearch");
}
?>

<tr><td><br/>
<a href="<?php echo
$_SERVER['PHP_SELF']."?viewall=viewall"; ?>">View list</a>
</td></tr>
<tr><td>
<a href="<?php echo $_SERVER['PHP_SELF']; ?>">Main Menu</a>
```

5.5 Step 5: The User Profile

The user profile page generated by the admin script not only displays user information, it can also update user information or delete a user. The profile page functionality is actually the bulk of the code for the admin script. When a userid is passed into the admin script via the uid variable, the script checks to see if the delete or update buttons were clicked.

If the delete button is clicked, the userid is used in an SQL statement to delete the user. This action takes place immediately; there is no confirmation check to verify that the administrator truly means to delete the user. It would be a good idea to add a confirmation step before deletion.

If the update button is clicked, the userid is used in several SQL statements to update user information. If a new email address is entered for the user and the rest of the user information does not change, then only an SQL statement updating the email column for the user is executed. If the user's password in changed in addition to the email address, then that SQL statement is also executed. Error checking is performed on the new password or email to make sure they are valid. If there are no errors the user information is updated.

If neither, the delete or update, button is clicked, the user information is displayed in a form. The form displays the current user information stored in the user table, with fields to enter new information. At the end of the form, the administrator has the option of clicking on the update button or the delete button.

CODE

MySQL

```
// if passed the userid, take one of several actions, after
pulling up the user profile

elseif ($uid):

// if the delete button is pressed, delete user
if($_POST['deleteuser']){

$delete = mysql_query("delete from user WHERE id=$uid");
?>
<tr><td align=left colspan=3 valign=top width=500><b>
<? print("User has been deleted"); ?>
</b></td></tr>

<tr><td><br/>
<a href="<? echo $_SERVER['PHP_SELF']."?viewall=viewall";
?>">View list</a>
</td></tr>
<tr><td>
<a href="<? echo $_SERVER['PHP_SELF']; ?>">Main Menu</a>
<?
}

// if new information is submitted, update the user
information
else{
if ($_POST['submit']) {
if($_POST['newpassword'] !=''){
if (!ereg("^[A-Za-z0-9]{4,12}$",$_POST['newpassword'])){
$err ="<tr>
<td align=left colspan=3 valign=top width=356><b>
Your <font color=\"#9c2108\">Password</font>:
<br/>-must be 4-12 characters long<br/>-can contain numbers
```

```
<br/>-cannot contain spaces<br/>-cannot contain non-
alphanumeric symbols such as \".?!#@$%*&\"
</b></td></tr>\n";
}
else {
$_POST['newpassword'] = md5($_POST['newpassword']);
//encrypt password
$sql = "UPDATE user SET
password='".$_POST['newpassword']."' WHERE id=$uid";
$result = mysql_query($sql);
}
}


/*
//if your user table stored firstname and lastname, you
would also update them if necessary
$sql3 = "UPDATE user SET lastname='".$_POST['lastname']. "'
WHERE id=$uid";
$sql2 = "UPDATE user SET firstname='".$_POST['firstname'].
"' WHERE id=$uid";
*/

if($_POST['newemail'] !=''){
if(!ereg('^[-!#$%&\'*+\\./0-9=?A-Z^_`a-z{|}~]+'.
'@'.
'[-!#$%&\'*+\\/0-9=?A-Z^_`a-z{|}~]+\.'.
'[-!#$%&\'*+\\./0-9=?A-Z^_`a-z{|}~]+$',
$_POST['newemail'])){
$err .= "<tr>
 <td align=left colspan=3 valign=top width=500><b>
Your <font color=\"#9c2108\">E-mail address </font>
is not valid. </b></td></tr>\n";
}
else {
$sql1= "UPDATE user SET email='".$_POST['newemail']."'
WHERE id=$uid";
$result1 = mysql_query($sql1);
}
}
```

```php
/*
//if your user table stored firstname and lastname, you
would also update them if necessary
$result3 = mysql_query($sql3);
$result2 = mysql_query($sql2);
*/

if(!$err){

?>
 <tr><td align=left colspan=3 valign=top width=500><b>Thank
you! Information updated:</b>
<br/><br/>

<a href="<? echo $_SERVER['PHP_SELF']."?uid=$uid"; ?>">View
updated record</a></td></tr>
<?
}
else {
print ("$err");
print ("<tr><td align=left colspan=3 valign=top width=500>
<a href=\"".$_SERVER['PHP_SELF']."?uid=$uid\">
Go Back.</a></td></tr>");
}
?>

<tr><td><br/>
<a href="<? echo $_SERVER['PHP_SELF']."?viewall=viewall";
?>">View list</a>
</td></tr>
<tr><td>
<a href="<? echo $_SERVER['PHP_SELF']; ?>">Main Menu</a>
<?

} else {

// display the user profile
```

```php
// query the DB
$sql = "SELECT * FROM user WHERE id=$uid";
$result = mysql_query($sql);
$myrow = mysql_fetch_array($result);
?>

<p><b>
<font color="#9c2108">member: <? echo $myrow["username"];
?></font>
</b></p>

<br/>

<form method="post" action="<?php echo
$_SERVER['SCRIPT_NAME']; ?>">
<input type=hidden name="uid" value="<?php echo
$myrow["id"]; ?>">

<table border="0" cellpadding="1" cellspacing="0">
<tr>
<td align=left width=150>Username :</td>
<td align=left width=350>
<?php echo $myrow["username"] ?> </td></tr>
<tr>
<td align=left>Present Password :</td>
 <td align=left>
  <?php echo $myrow["password"] ?></td></tr>
<tr>
<td align=left>New password? :</td>
<td align=left><input type="password" name="newpassword"
value="">
</td></tr>

<!-- if your user table stored firstname and lastname, you
would output the stored values in fields for update
<tr>
<td align=left>First Name :</td>
<td align=left>
```

```
<input type="Text" name="firstname" value="<?php echo
$myrow["firstname"]; ?>">
</td></tr>
<tr>
<td align=left>Last Name :</td>
<td align=left>
<input type="Text" name="lastname" value="<?php echo
$myrow["lastname"]; ?>">
</td></tr>
-->

<tr>
 <td align=left>Email Address :</td>
 <td align=left><?php echo $myrow["email"]; ?></td></tr>
<tr>
<td align=left>New Email Address? :</td>
<td align=left><input type="Text" name="newemail" value="">
</td></tr>

<!-- if your user table stored last login time and date
registered  you can output the stored values
<tr><td align=left>
Last Login:</td>
<td align=left> <?php print $myrow["last_login"];
?></td></tr>
<tr><td align=left>Account created:</td>
<td align=left> <?php echo $myrow["registered"];
?></td></tr>
-->

<tr><td>
<br>
<input type="Submit" name="submit" value="Update
information">
<br/><br/>
<input type="Submit" name="deleteuser" value="Delete User">
</td></tr>

<?php
```

```php
$referer = isset($_SERVER['HTTP_REFERER']) ?
$_SERVER['HTTP_REFERER'] : '' ; // assign '' or any default
value;
if (!$referer == '') {
echo '<tr><td><br/><a href="' . $referer . '" title="Return
to the previous page">&laquo; Go back</a></td></tr>';
} else {
echo '<tr><td><br/><a href="javascript:history.go(-1)"
title="Return to the previous page">&laquo; Go
back</a></td></tr>';
}
?>
<tr><td><br/>
<a href="<? echo $_SERVER['PHP_SELF']."?viewall=viewall";
?>">View list</a>
</td></tr>

<tr><td>
<a href="<?php  echo $_SERVER['PHP_SELF']; ?>">Main
Menu</a>
</td></tr>
</form>
</table>

<?php
}
}
```

OUTPUT

Logged in as: admin - [ADMIN]

member: summer23

Username :   summer23
Present Password :   d3c9574bf0a801eed5857a220414d16c
New password? :   [   ]
Email Address :
New Email Address? : [   ]

[Update information]

[Delete User]

« Go back

View list
Main Menu

Logout

MySQLi Procedural

```
// if passed the userid, take one of several actions, after
pulling up the user profile

} elseif ($uid){

// if the delete button is pressed, delete user
if(isset($_POST['deleteuser'])){

$delete = mysqli_query($con, "delete from user WHERE
id=$uid");
?>
...
<?php
}

// if new information is submitted, update the user
information
else{
...

$_POST['newpassword'] = md5($_POST['newpassword']);
//encrypt password
$sql = "UPDATE user SET
password='".mysqli_real_escape_string($con,
$_POST['newpassword'])."' WHERE id='$uid'";
$result = mysqli_query($con, $sql);
}
}

/*
//if your user table stored firstname and lastname, you
would also update them if necessary
$sql3 = "UPDATE user SET lastname='".$_POST['lastname']. "'
WHERE id=$uid";
$sql2 = "UPDATE user SET firstname='".$_POST['firstname'].
"' WHERE id=$uid";
```

```php
*/

if($_POST['newemail'] !=''){
…

$sql1= "UPDATE user SET
email='".mysqli_real_escape_string($con,
$_POST['newemail'])."' WHERE id='$uid'";
$result1 = mysqli_query($con, $sql1);
}
}

/*
//if your user table stored firstname and lastname, you
would also update them if necessary
$result3 = mysqli_query($con, $sql3);
$result2 = mysqli_query($con, $sql2);
*/

…

if(!$err){
…
  } else {

// display the user profile

    // query the DB

    $sql = "SELECT * FROM user WHERE id='$uid'";
    //echo "$sql<br/>";
    $result = mysqli_query($con, $sql);
    $myrow = mysqli_fetch_array($result);

  // echo mysqli_error();
    ?>

<p>
<b>
```

```
<font color="#9c2108">member: <?php echo
$myrow["username"]; ?></font>
</b>
</p>

...
}
```

MySQLi Object-Oriented

```
// if passed the userid, take one of several actions, after
pulling up the user profile

} elseif ($uid){

// if the delete button is pressed, delete user
if(isset($_POST['deleteuser'])){

$delete = $con->query("delete from user WHERE id=$uid");
?>
...
<?php
}

// if new information is submitted, update the user
information
else{
...

$_POST['newpassword'] = md5($_POST['newpassword']);
//encrypt password
$sql = "UPDATE user SET password='".$con-
>real_escape_string($_POST['newpassword'])."' WHERE
id='$uid'";
$result = $con->query($sql);}
}

/*
//if your user table stored firstname and lastname, you
would also update them if necessary
$sql3 = "UPDATE user SET lastname="'.$_POST['lastname']. "'
WHERE id=$uid";
$sql2 = "UPDATE user SET firstname='".$_POST['firstname'].
"' WHERE id=$uid";
*/
```

```php
if($_POST['newemail'] !=''){
...

$sql1= "UPDATE user SET email='".$con-
>real_escape_string($_POST['newemail'])."' WHERE
id='$uid'";
$result1 = $con->query($sql1);}
}

/*
//if your user table stored firstname and lastname, you
would also update them if necessary
$result3 = $con->query($sql3);
$result2 = $con->query($sql2);
*/

...

if(!$err){
...
   } else {

// display the user profile

    // query the DB

    $sql = "SELECT * FROM user WHERE id='$uid'";
    //echo "$sql<br/>";
    $result = mysqli_query($con, $sql);
    $myrow = mysqli_fetch_array($result);

   // echo mysqli_error();
    ?>

<p>
<b>
<font color="#9c2108">member: <?php echo
$myrow["username"]; ?></font>
</b>
```

```
</p>

...
}
```

PHP Data Object

```php
// if passed the userid, take one of several actions, after
pulling up the user profile

} elseif ($uid){

// if the delete button is pressed, delete user
if(isset($_POST['deleteuser'])){

try{
$delete = $con->prepare("delete from user WHERE id = ?");
$delete->bindParam(1, $uid, PDO::PARAM_INT);
$delete->execute();
}
 catch (PDOException $e)
{
     $error = 'Error: ' . $e->getMessage();
     echo $error;
     //exit();
}

?>
...
<?php
}

// if new information is submitted, update the user
information
else{
...
$_POST['newpassword'] = md5($_POST['newpassword']);
//encrypt password

try{
$sql = "UPDATE user SET password = ? WHERE id = ?";
$changerecord1 = $con->prepare($sql);
```

```php
$changerecord1->bindParam(1, $_POST['newpassword'],
PDO::PARAM_STR);
$changerecord1->bindParam(2, $uid, PDO::PARAM_INT);
$changerecord1->execute();
}
 catch (PDOException $e)
{
     $error = 'Error: ' . $e->getMessage();
     echo $error;
     //exit();
}


}
}

if($_POST['newemail'] !=''){
…

try{
$sql1= "UPDATE user SET email = ? WHERE id = ?";
$changerecord2= $con->prepare($sql1);
$changerecord2->bindParam(1, $_POST['newemail'],
PDO::PARAM_STR);
$changerecord2->bindParam(2, $uid, PDO::PARAM_INT);
$changerecord2->execute();
}
 catch (PDOException $e)
{
     $error = 'Error: ' . $e->getMessage();
     echo $error;
     //exit();
}


}
}

/*
//if your user table stored firstname and lastname, you
would also update them if necessary
```

```
try{
$sql3 = "UPDATE user SET lastname = ? WHERE id = ?";
$changerecord3 = $con->prepare($sql3);
$changerecord3->bindParam(1, $_POST['lastname'],
PDO::PARAM_STR);
$changerecord3->bindParam(2, $uid, PDO::PARAM_INT);
$changerecord3->execute();
}
 catch (PDOException $e)
{
    $error = 'Error: ' . $e->getMessage();
    echo $error;
    //exit();
}

try{
$sql4 = "UPDATE user SET firstname = ? WHERE id = ?";
$changerecord4 = $con->prepare($sql4);
$changerecord4->bindParam(1, $_POST['firstname'],
PDO::PARAM_STR);
$changerecord4->bindParam(2, $uid, PDO::PARAM_INT);
$changerecord4->execute();
}
 catch (PDOException $e)
{
    $error = 'Error: ' . $e->getMessage();
    echo $error;
    //exit();
}
*/

if(!$err){
...
   } else {

// display the user profile

    // query the DB
```

```php
$sql = "SELECT * FROM user WHERE id = ?";

    try{
    $result = $con->prepare($sql);
    $result->bindParam(1, $uid, PDO::PARAM_INT);
     $result->execute();

     /* bind result variables */
    $result->bindColumn(1, $id);
    //bind additional results if needed
    $result->bindColumn(2, $username);
    $result->bindColumn(3, $password);
    $result->bindColumn(4, $email);
    $result->bindColumn(5, $level);
          }
     catch (PDOException $e)
    {
     $error = 'Error: ' . $e->getMessage();
         echo $error;
         //exit();
    }

         $result->fetch();
    ?>
```

5.6 The complete "admin.php" script

CODE

MySQL

```php
<?php
session_start();

require( 'database.php' );

if (!$_SESSION['loggedin']) {
   die("Not logged in"); //this causes to script to stop
executing and lets the user know there is a problem

/*
Note:  instead of the die() function, you could use the
echo() function and provide an HTML link back to the login
page, or use the header() function to just redirect users
to the login page without any message. It is up to you to
decide how your application should function.
*/
}

elseif ($_SESSION['loggedin'] &&
($_SESSION['adminuser']=='0') ){  //logged in and NOT an
Admin
die("You do not have the right privileges to access this
page");
}

elseif ($_SESSION['loggedin'] &&
($_SESSION['adminuser']=='1') ){  //logged in and an Admin
```

```php
/* what a user would be able to do if logged in and the
Admin. It is up to you to decide how your application
should function. */
echo "Logged in as: {$_SESSION['loggedinuser']} -
[ADMIN]<br/><br/>\n";

?>

<table border="0" cellpadding="3" cellspacing="0"
width="500">
  <tr><td align="left" valign="top" width="500">

<?php

 // count users
$totalquery = mysql_query("SELECT id FROM user");
$total = mysql_num_rows($totalquery);

//sets the values for the variables regardless of GET/POST
method
if(isset($_POST['viewall'])){
    $viewall = $_POST['viewall'];
} else {
if(isset($_GET['viewall'])){
    $viewall = $_GET['viewall'];
}}

if(isset($_GET['let'])){
    $let = mysql_real_escape_string($_GET['let']);
}

if(isset($_POST['finduser'])){
    $finduser = $_POST['finduser'];
}else {
if(isset($_GET['finduser'])){
    $finduser = $_GET['finduser'];
}}

if(isset($_POST['searchwords'])){
```

```php
    $searchwords =
mysql_real_escape_string($_POST['searchwords']);
}else {
if(isset($_GET['searchwords'])){
    $searchwords = $_GET['searchwords'];
}}

if(isset($_GET['uid'])){
    $uid=mysql_real_escape_string($_GET['uid']);
} else {
if(isset($_POST['uid'])){
    $uid = mysql_real_escape_string($_POST['uid']);
}}

//Set this to the number of records per page
$limit = 5;

if(isset($_GET['offset'])){
    $offset=mysql_real_escape_string($_GET['offset']);
}
else{
//Set the initial offset
if (!isset($offset)) $offset = 0;
}

// search for users by the first letter in username

if ($let):
$letter_total= mysql_query("select id,username from user
where username like '$let%'");
$numrows_letter= mysql_num_rows($letter_total);

$letter= mysql_query("select id,username from user where
username like '$let%'
        LIMIT $offset, $limit");

  if (mysql_num_rows($letter)>0) {
        $numrows= mysql_num_rows($letter);
        $x=0;
```

```
        while ($x<$numrows){
            $id= mysql_result($letter,$x, id);
    $username= mysql_result($letter,$x, username);
printf("<a href=\"%s?uid=%s\">%s</a><br/>\n",
$_SERVER['PHP_SELF'],$id, $username);
            $x++;


        }
//print "<br/>". get_nav_letter($offset, $limit,
$numrows_letter);
print "<br/>". get_nav($offset, $limit,
$numrows_letter,"letter");

?>
</td></tr>
<tr><td>
<a href="<?php echo
$_SERVER['PHP_SELF']."?viewall=viewall"; ?>">View list</a>
</td></tr>
<tr><td>
<a href="<?php echo $_SERVER['PHP_SELF']; ?>">Main Menu</a>
<?
    }
else{
print "<tr><td align=left colSpan=3 valign=top width=500>
    No records found for letter <b>$let</b></td></tr>";
?>
<tr><td><br/>
<a href="<?php echo
$_SERVER['PHP_SELF']."?viewall=viewall"; ?>">View list</a>
</td></tr>
<tr><td>
<a href="<?php echo $_SERVER['PHP_SELF']; ?>">Main Menu</a>
<?
    }

// if passed searchwords

elseif ($finduser):
```

```php
if (!ereg("[[:alnum:]]",$searchwords)):
echo "<p>Your <font color=\"#FF0000\"><b>search</b></font>
must be alphanumeric characters.";
echo "<br/>Letters a-z and numbers 0-9.</p>";

else:

//add or remove fields to search to array
$fieldstosearch = array("username","email");

for($i=0;$i<count($fieldstosearch);$i++) {
$clause .= sprintf("(%s LIKE '%%%s%%') OR ",
$fieldstosearch[$i], urldecode($searchwords));
}
//use substring function to remove last four characters
from clause
if(count($fieldstosearch) > 1) {
$clause = "(".substr($clause, 0, -4).")";
}
else {
$clause = substr($clause, 0, -4);

}
//print field(s) query, this is optional
print $clause."<p>";

$searchq = mysql_query("SELECT id from user WHERE
$clause");
$numrows_search = mysql_num_rows($searchq);

$realsql = "SELECT * from user WHERE $clause LIMIT $offset,
$limit";
$result = mysql_query($realsql);
if (mysql_num_rows($result) > 0) {
$itemnum=$offset+1;
while($row = mysql_fetch_array($result)) {
printf("%s <a href=\"%s?uid=%s\">%s</a><br/>\n",
$itemnum++, $_SERVER['PHP_SELF'],
```

```
$row["id"], $row["username"]);
}
}
else {
print "Sorry No records found";
}

print "<br/>". get_nav($offset, $limit, $numrows_search,
"usersearch");

endif;
?>

<tr><td><br/>
<a href="<? echo $_SERVER['PHP_SELF']."?viewall=viewall";
?>">View list</a>
</td></tr>
<tr><td>
<a href="<? echo $_SERVER['PHP_SELF']; ?>">Main Menu</a>

<?php
// if passed the userid take of of several actions after
pulling up user profile
elseif ($uid):

// if the delete button is pressed, delete user
if($_POST['deleteuser']){

$delete = mysql_query("delete from user WHERE id=$uid");
?>
<tr><td align=left colspan=3 valign=top width=500><b>
<? print("User has been deleted"); ?>
</b></td></tr>

<tr><td><br/>
<a href="<? echo $_SERVER['PHP_SELF']."?viewall=viewall";
?>">View list</a>
</td></tr>
<tr><td>
```

```php
<a href="<? echo $_SERVER['PHP_SELF']; ?>">Main Menu</a>
<?
}

// if new information is submitted, update the user
information
else{
if ($_POST['submit']) {
if($_POST['newpassword'] !=''){
if (!ereg("^[A-Za-z0-9]{4,12}$",$_POST['newpassword'])){
$err ="<tr>
<td align=left colspan=3 valign=top width=356><b>
Your <font color=\"#9c2108\">Password</font>:
<br/>-must be 4-12 characters long<br/>-can contain numbers
<br/>-cannot contain spaces<br/>-cannot contain non-
alphanumeric symbols such as \".?!#@$%*&\"
</b></td></tr>\n";}
else{
$_POST['newpassword'] = md5($_POST['newpassword']);
//encrypt password
$sql = "UPDATE user SET
password='".mysql_real_escape_string($_POST['newpassword'])
."' WHERE id=$uid";
$result = mysql_query($sql);
}
}

/*
//if your user table stored firstname and lastname, you
would also update them if necessary
$sql3 = "UPDATE user SET lastname='".$_POST['lastname']. "'
WHERE id=$uid";
$sql2 = "UPDATE user SET firstname='".$_POST['firstname'].
"' WHERE id=$uid";
*/

if($_POST['newemail'] !=''){
if(!ereg('^[-!#$%&\'*+\\./0-9=?A-Z^_`a-z{|}~]+'.
'@'.
```

```php
'[-!#$%&\'*+\\/0-9=?A-Z^_`a-z{|}~]+\.'.
'[-!#$%&\'*+\\./0-9=?A-Z^_`a-z{|}~]+$',
$_POST['newemail'])){
 $err .= "<tr>
 <td align=left colspan=3 valign=top width=500><b>
 Your <font color=\"#9c2108\">E-mail address </font>
 is not valid. </b></td></tr>\n";}
else{
$sql1= "UPDATE user SET
email='".mysql_real_escape_string($_POST['newemail'])."'
WHERE id=$uid";
$result1 = mysql_query($sql1);
}
}

/*
//if your user table stored firstname and lastname, you
would also update them if necessary
$result3 = mysql_query($sql3);
$result2 = mysql_query($sql2);
*/


if(!$err){

?>
 <tr><td align=left colspan=3 valign=top width=500><b>Thank
you! Information updated:</b>
<br/><br/>

<a href="<? echo $_SERVER['PHP_SELF']."?uid=$uid"; ?>">View
updated record</a></td></tr>
<?
}
else{
print ("$err");
print ("<tr><td align=left colspan=3 valign=top width=500>
<a href=\"".$_SERVER['PHP_SELF']."?uid=$uid\">
Go Back.</a></td></tr>");
```

```php
}
?>

<tr><td><br/>
<a href="<? echo $_SERVER['PHP_SELF']."?viewall=viewall";
?>">View list</a>
</td></tr>
<tr><td>
<a href="<? echo $_SERVER['PHP_SELF']; ?>">Main Menu</a>
<?

  } else {

// display the user profile

    // query the DB

    $sql = "SELECT * FROM user WHERE id=$uid";
    //echo "$sql<br/>";
    $result = mysql_query($sql);
    $myrow = mysql_fetch_array($result);

  // echo mysql_error();
    ?>

<p>
<b>
<font color="#9c2108">member: <? echo $myrow["username"];
?></font>
</b>
</p>

<br/>

<form method="post" action="<?php echo
$_SERVER['SCRIPT_NAME']; ?>">
<input type=hidden name="uid" value="<?php echo
$myrow["id"]; ?>">
```

```
<table border="0" cellpadding="1" cellspacing="0">
        <tr>
            <td align=left width=150>Username :</td>
            <td align=left width=350>
            <?php echo $myrow["username"] ?> </td></tr>
            <tr>
            <td align=left>Present Password :</td>
 <td align=left>
 <?php echo $myrow["password"] ?></td></tr>
<tr>
            <td align=left>New password? :</td>
            <td align=left><input type="password"
name="newpassword" value="">
</td></tr>
<!-- if your user table stored firstname and lastname, you
would output the stored values in fields for update
<tr>
            <td align=left>First Name :</td>
            <td align=left>
<input type="Text" name="firstname" value="<?php echo
$myrow["firstname"]; ?>">
</td></tr>
        <tr>
            <td align=left>Last Name :</td>
            <td align=left>
<input type="Text" name="lastname" value="<?php echo
$myrow["lastname"]; ?>">
</td></tr>
-->
        <tr>
            <td align=left>Email Address :</td>
            <td align=left><?php echo $myrow["email"];
?></td></tr>
<tr>
    <td align=left>New Email Address? :</td>
    <td align=left><input type="Text" name="newemail"
value="">
</td></tr>
```

```
<!--
<tr><td align=left>
Last Login:</td>
<td align=left> <?php print $myrow["last_login"];
?></td></tr>
<tr><td align=left>Account created:</td>
<td align=left> <?php echo $myrow["registered"];
?></td></tr>
-->
<tr><td>
<br>
<input type="Submit" name="submit" value="Update
information">
<br/><br/>
<input type="Submit" name="deleteuser" value="Delete User">
</td></tr>

<?php
$referer = $_SERVER['HTTP_REFERER'];
    if (!$referer == '') {
        echo '<tr><td><br/><a href="' . $referer . '"
title="Return to the previous page">&laquo; Go
back</a></td></tr>';
    } else {
        echo '<tr><td><br/><a href="javascript:history.go(-
1)" title="Return to the previous page">&laquo; Go
back</a></td></tr>';
    }
?>
<tr><td><br/>
<a href="<? echo $_SERVER['PHP_SELF']."?viewall=viewall";
?>">View list</a>
</td></tr>

<tr><td>
<a href="<?php  echo $_SERVER['PHP_SELF']; ?>">Main
Menu</a>
</td></tr>
    </form>
```

```php
</table>

<?php
}
}

// show a list of all users

elseif($viewall):

 // display list of users
$result_all = mysql_query("SELECT id,username FROM user
order by username LIMIT $offset, $limit");

print("There are currently <b>$total</b> Users.");
print("<br/><br/>\n");

while ($myrow = mysql_fetch_array($result_all)) {
printf("<a href=\"%s?uid=%s\">%s</a><br/>\n",
$_SERVER['PHP_SELF'],
$myrow["id"], $myrow["username"]);
}

print "<br/>". get_nav($offset, $limit, $total);

?>
</td></tr>

<tr><td><br/>
<a href="<?php echo
$_SERVER['PHP_SELF']."?viewall=viewall"; ?>">View list</a>
</td></tr>

<tr><td>
<a href="<?php echo $_SERVER['PHP_SELF']; ?>">Main Menu</a>
<?

// main page of user admin application
```

```php
else:

print "";
print("There are currently <b>$total</b> Users.");
print("<br/><br/>\n");
print "Search by letter<p>";

for ($i = 65 ; $i < 91 ; $i++){

// if $i is non-zero and is divisible by 5 print a line
break.
//# Create a new row every five columns
if (($i % 5 == 0) && ($i!=0)){
 echo "<br />";
}
//# Add a column
printf ('<a href = "%s?let=%s">%s</a> ',
$_SERVER['PHP_SELF'], chr($i+32), chr($i));
}

?>
<br/><br/>
<form method="post" action="<?php echo
$_SERVER['SCRIPT_NAME']; ?>">
Search for: <input type="text" name="searchwords"
value=""><br>
<input type="submit" name="finduser" value="Find User">
</form>

<br/><br/> Or View all Users
<form method="post" action="<?php echo
$_SERVER['SCRIPT_NAME']; ?>">
<input type=submit name="viewall" value="Viewall">
</form>

<?php
endif;
?>
</td></tr>
```

```
</table>

<?php

echo "<p><a href=\"logout.php\">Logout</a></p>";
}

function get_nav($offset, $limit, $totalnum, $type =
"normal") {
$navigation ='';

    if ($totalnum > $limit) {

//sprintf() returns the result as a formatted string vs
//printf() outputs the result as a formatted string
//if you use printf instead of sprintf in the function you
will notice a number
//being output along with everything else, this is because
printf returns
//the length of the outputted string.

 $navigation  .= sprintf('<table><tr><td>');
    // Print File # - # of # (Customize to your need here)
 $navigation  .= sprintf('Record(s) %s', ( $offset + 1 ));
     $navigation  .= sprintf(' - ');
   if( $offset + $limit >= $totalnum ){
     $navigation  .= sprintf($totalnum);
   }else{ $navigation  .= sprintf ( $offset + $limit ); }
$navigation  .= sprintf(' of %s      |    </td>', $totalnum);

$navigation  .= sprintf('<td>Page </td>',"\n");

//print previous
if ($offset != 0) {
    $boffset = $offset-$limit;
if($type=='letter'){
$navigation .= sprintf('<td><a
href="%s?let=%s&offset=%s"><<</a></td>',
        $_SERVER['PHP_SELF'],$GLOBALS['let'],$boffset);
```

```php
}elseif($type =='usersearch'){
$navigation .= sprintf('<td><a
href="%s?finduser=yes&offset=%s&searchwords=%s"><<</a></td>
',

$_SERVER['PHP_SELF'],$boffset,urlencode($GLOBALS['searchwor
ds']));
}
else{
$navigation .= sprintf('<td><a
href="%s?viewall=viewall&offset=%s"><<</a></td>',
$_SERVER['PHP_SELF'],$boffset);
}
}

// calculate number of pages needing links
$pages = intval($totalnum/$limit);

// $pages now contains int of pages needed unless there is
a remainder from division
if ($totalnum%$limit) $pages++;

//print pages
for ($i=1; $i <= $pages; $i++) { // loop thru
$newoffset=$limit*($i-1);
if ($newoffset != $offset) {
if($type=='letter'){
$navigation .= sprintf('<td><a
href="%s?let=%s&offset=%s">%s</a></td>%s',
        $_SERVER['PHP_SELF'], $GLOBALS['let'], $newoffset,
$i, "\n");
}
elseif($type =='usersearch'){
$navigation .= sprintf('<td><a
href="%s?finduser=yes&offset=%s&searchwords=%s">%s</a></td>
%s',
    $_SERVER['PHP_SELF'],
$newoffset,urlencode($GLOBALS['searchwords']), $i, "\n");
}
```

```php
else{
$navigation .= sprintf('<td><a
href="%s?viewall=viewall&offset=%s">%s</a></td>%s',
$_SERVER['PHP_SELF'], $newoffset, $i, "\n");
}
}
else {
$navigation .= sprintf('<td>%s</td>%s', $i, "\n");
}
}

//print next
$noffset = $pages*$limit-$limit;
if ($offset != $noffset)
{
    $boffset = $offset+$limit;
if($type=='letter'){
$navigation .= sprintf('<td><a
href="%s?let=%s&offset=%s">>></a></td>',
        $_SERVER['PHP_SELF'], $GLOBALS['let'], $boffset);
}
elseif($type =='usersearch'){
$navigation .= sprintf('<td><a
href="%s?finduser=yes&offset=%s&searchwords=%s">>></a></td>
',
        $_SERVER['PHP_SELF'],
$boffset,urlencode($GLOBALS['searchwords']));
}
else{
$navigation .= sprintf('<td><a
href="%s?viewall=viewall&offset=%s">>></a></td>',
        $_SERVER['PHP_SELF'], $boffset);
}
}
$navigation .= sprintf('</tr></table>');
}

else {
$navigation = "";
```

```php
    }

    return $navigation;
}

?>
```

MySQLi Procedural

```php
<?php
session_start();

date_default_timezone_set("America/New_York");

error_reporting(E_ALL);
ini_set('display_errors', '1');

require( 'database.php' );

if (!isset($_SESSION['loggedin'])) {
   die("Not logged in"); //this causes to script to stop
executing and lets the user know there is a problem

/*
Note:  instead of the die() function, you could use the
echo() function and provide an HTML link back to the login
page, or use the header() function to just redirect users
to the login page without any message. It is up to you to
decide how your application should function.
*/
}

elseif (isset($_SESSION['loggedin']) &&
($_SESSION['adminuser']=='0') ){  //logged in and NOT an
Admin
die("You do not have the right privileges to access this
page");
}

elseif (isset($_SESSION['loggedin']) &&
($_SESSION['adminuser']=='1') ){  //logged in and an Admin

/* what a user would be able to do if logged in and the
Admin. It is up to you to decide how your application
should function. */
```

```php
echo "Logged in as: {$_SESSION['loggedinuser']} -
[ADMIN]<br/><br/>\n";

?>

<table border="0" cellpadding="3" cellspacing="0"
width="500">
  <tr><td align="left" valign="top" width="500">

<?php
//setup variables

$let = '' ; // assign default value
$finduser = '' ; // assign default value
$uid = '' ; // assign default value
$viewall = '' ; // assign default value
$searchwords = '' ; // assign default value
$id = '' ; // assign default value
$username = '' ; // assign default value
$err = '' ; // assign default value
$clause = '' ; // assign default value

//count users
$totalquery = mysqli_query($con, "SELECT id FROM user");
$total = mysqli_num_rows($totalquery);

//sets the values for the variables regardless of GET/POST
method
if(isset($_POST['viewall'])){
    $viewall = $_POST['viewall'];
} else {
if(isset($_GET['viewall'])){
    $viewall = $_GET['viewall'];
}}

if(isset($_GET['let'])){
//echo "<p>1 - {$_GET['let']}</p>";
```

```php
//mysqli_real_escape_string requires two variables; the
connection variable, and the string variable.
$let = mysqli_real_escape_string($con, $_GET['let']);

//echo "<p>2 - $let</p>";
}

if(isset($_POST['finduser'])){
    $finduser = $_POST['finduser'];
}else {
if(isset($_GET['finduser'])){
    $finduser = $_GET['finduser'];
}}

if(isset($_POST['searchwords'])){
    $searchwords = $con-
>real_escape_string($_POST['searchwords']);
}else {
if(isset($_GET['searchwords'])){
    $searchwords = $_GET['searchwords'];
}}

if(isset($_GET['uid'])){
    $uid=mysqli_real_escape_string($con, $_GET['uid']);
} else {
if(isset($_POST['uid'])){
    $uid = mysqli_real_escape_string($con, $_POST['uid']);
}}

//Set this to the number of records per page
$limit = 5;

if(isset($_GET['offset'])){
    $offset=mysqli_real_escape_string($con,
$_GET['offset']);
}
else{
//Set the initial offset
if (!isset($offset)) $offset = 0;
```

```php
}

// search for users by the first letter in username

if ($let){
$letter_total= mysqli_query($con, "select id,username from
user where username like '$let%'");
$numrows_letter= mysqli_num_rows($letter_total);

$letter= mysqli_query($con, "select id,username from user
where username like '$let%'
        LIMIT $offset, $limit");

//there is no equivalent to mysql_result function

function mysqli_result($result, $iRow = 0, $sField = '')
{
    $return = false;
    if (mysqli_data_seek($result, $iRow))
    {
        $record = mysqli_fetch_array($result);
        if (empty($sField) && isset($record[0]))
        {
            $return = $record[0];
        }
        elseif (!empty($sField) && isset($record[$sField]))
        {
            $return = $record[$sField];
        }
    }
    return $return;
}


  if (mysqli_num_rows($letter)>0) {
      $row = mysqli_fetch_array($letter, MYSQLI_NUM);

    $numrows= mysqli_num_rows($letter);
```

```php
$x=0;

while ($x<$numrows){

$id= mysqli_result($letter,$x, 'id');
$username= mysqli_result($letter,$x, 'username');

printf("<a href=\"%s?uid=%s\">%s</a><br/>\n",
$_SERVER['PHP_SELF'],$id, $username);

$x++;

}

print "<br/>". get_nav($offset, $limit,
$numrows_letter,"letter");

?>
</td></tr>
<tr><td>
<a href="<?php echo
$_SERVER['PHP_SELF']."?viewall=viewall"; ?>">View list</a>
</td></tr>
<tr><td>
<a href="<?php echo $_SERVER['PHP_SELF']; ?>">Main Menu</a>
<?php
}
else{
print "<tr><td align=left colSpan=3 valign=top width=500>
    No records found for letter <b>$let</b></td></tr>";
?>
<tr><td><br/>
<a href="<?php echo
$_SERVER['PHP_SELF']."?viewall=viewall"; ?>">View list</a>
</td></tr>
<tr><td>
<a href="<?php echo $_SERVER['PHP_SELF']; ?>">Main Menu</a>
<?php
```

```php
    }

// if passed searchwords, try to find matching user(s)
} elseif ($finduser){

//if (!ereg("[[:alnum:]]",$searchwords)):
if (!preg_match('/[[:alnum:]]/i', $searchwords)){
echo "<p>Your <font color=\"#FF0000\"><b>search</b></font>
must be alphanumeric characters.";
echo "<br/>Letters a-z and numbers 0-9.</p>";

} else {

//add or remove fields to search to array
$fieldstosearch = array("username","email");

for($i=0;$i<count($fieldstosearch);$i++) {
$clause .= sprintf("(%s LIKE '%%%s%%') OR ",
$fieldstosearch[$i], urldecode($searchwords));
}
//use substring function to remove last four characters
from clause
if(count($fieldstosearch) > 1) {
$clause = "(".substr($clause, 0, -4).")";
}
else {
$clause = substr($clause, 0, -4);

}
//print field(s) query, this is optional
print $clause."<p>";

$searchq = mysqli_query($con, "SELECT id from user WHERE
$clause");
$numrows_search = mysqli_num_rows($searchq);

$realsql = "SELECT * from user WHERE $clause LIMIT $offset,
$limit";
$result = mysqli_query($con, $realsql);
```

```php
if (mysqli_num_rows($result) > 0) {
$itemnum=$offset+1;
while($row = mysqli_fetch_array($result)) {
printf("%s <a href=\"%s?uid=%s\">%s</a><br/>\n",
$itemnum++, $_SERVER['PHP_SELF'],
$row["id"], $row["username"]);
}
}
else {
print "Sorry No records found";
}


print "<br/>". get_nav($offset, $limit, $numrows_search,
"usersearch");


}
?>


<tr><td><br/>
<a href="<?php echo
$_SERVER['PHP_SELF']."?viewall=viewall"; ?>">View list</a>
</td></tr>
<tr><td>
<a href="<?php echo $_SERVER['PHP_SELF']; ?>">Main Menu</a>

<?php
// if passed the userid take one of several actions after
pulling up user profile
} elseif ($uid){

// if the delete button is pressed, delete user
if(isset($_POST['deleteuser'])){

$delete = mysqli_query($con, "delete from user WHERE
id=$uid");
?>
<tr><td align=left colspan=3 valign=top width=500><b>
<?php print("User has been deleted"); ?>
</b></td></tr>
```

```php
<tr><td><br/>
<a href="<?php echo
$_SERVER['PHP_SELF']."?viewall=viewall"; ?>">View list</a>
</td></tr>
<tr><td>
<a href="<?php echo $_SERVER['PHP_SELF']; ?>">Main Menu</a>
<?php
}

// if new information is submitted, update the user
information
else{
if (isset($_POST['submit'])) {

if($_POST['newpassword'] !=''){

//if (!ereg("^[A-Za-z0-9]{4,12}$",$_POST['newpassword'])){
if (!preg_match("/^[A-Za-z0-
9]{4,12}$/i",$_POST['newpassword'])){
$err ="<tr>
<td align=left colspan=3 valign=top width=356><b>
Your <font color=\"#9c2108\">Password</font>:
<br/>-must be 4-12 characters long<br/>-can contain numbers
<br/>-cannot contain spaces<br/>-cannot contain non-
alphanumeric symbols such as \".?!#@$%*&\"
</b></td></tr>\n";
}
else{
$_POST['newpassword'] = md5($_POST['newpassword']);
//encrypt password
$sql = "UPDATE user SET
password='".mysqli_real_escape_string($con,
$_POST['newpassword'])."' WHERE id='$uid'";
$result = mysqli_query($con, $sql);
}
}

/*
```

```
//if your user table stored firstname and lastname, you
would also update them if necessary
$sql3 = "UPDATE user SET lastname="'.$_POST['lastname']. "'
WHERE id=$uid";
$sql2 = "UPDATE user SET firstname='".$_POST['firstname'].
"' WHERE id=$uid";
*/


if($_POST['newemail'] !=''){
//use preg_match
//if(!preg_match('/^[[:alnum:]][a-z0-9_.-]*@[a-z0-9.-
]+\.[a-z]{2,4}$/i', $_POST['newemail'])){

//FILTER_VALIDATE_EMAIL filter validates value as an e-mail
address.
if(!filter_var($_POST['newemail'], FILTER_VALIDATE_EMAIL)){
 $err .= "<tr>
 <td align=left colspan=3 valign=top width=500><b>
 Your <font color=\"#9c2108\">E-mail address </font>
 is not valid. </b></td></tr>\n";}
else{
$sql1= "UPDATE user SET
email='".mysqli_real_escape_string($con,
$_POST['newemail'])."' WHERE id='$uid'";
$result1 = mysqli_query($con, $sql1);
}
}

/*
//if your user table stored firstname and lastname, you
would also update them if necessary
$result3 = mysqli_query($con, $sql3);
$result2 = mysqli_query($con, $sql2);
*/


if(!$err){

?>
```

```
 <tr><td align=left colspan=3 valign=top width=500><b>Thank
you! Information updated:</b>
<br/><br/>

<a href="<?php echo $_SERVER['PHP_SELF']."?uid=$uid";
?>">View updated record</a></td></tr>
<?php
}
else{
print ("$err");
print ("<tr><td align=left colspan=3 valign=top width=500>
<a href=\"".$_SERVER['PHP_SELF']."?uid=$uid\">
Go Back.</a></td></tr>");

}
?>


<tr><td><br/>
<a href="<?php echo
$_SERVER['PHP_SELF']."?viewall=viewall"; ?>">View list</a>
</td></tr>
<tr><td>
<a href="<?php echo $_SERVER['PHP_SELF']; ?>">Main Menu</a>
<?php

   } else {

// display the user profile

   // query the DB

   $sql = "SELECT * FROM user WHERE id='$uid'";
   //echo "$sql<br/>";
   $result = mysqli_query($con, $sql);
   $myrow = mysqli_fetch_array($result);

  // echo mysqli_error();
   ?>
```

```
<p>
<b>
<font color="#9c2108">member: <?php echo
$myrow["username"]; ?></font>
</b>
</p>

<br/>

<form method="post" action="<?php echo
$_SERVER['SCRIPT_NAME']; ?>">
<input type=hidden name="uid" value="<?php echo
$myrow["id"]; ?>">

<table border="0" cellpadding="1" cellspacing="0">
        <tr>
           <td align=left width=150>Username :</td>
           <td align=left width=350>
           <?php echo $myrow["username"] ?> </td></tr>
        <tr>
           <td align=left>Present Password :</td>
 <td align=left>
 <?php echo $myrow["password"] ?></td></tr>
<tr>
           <td align=left>New password? :</td>
           <td align=left><input type="password"
name="newpassword" value="">
</td></tr>
<!-- if your user table stored firstname and lastname, you
would output the stored values in fields for update
<tr>
           <td align=left>First Name :</td>
           <td align=left>
<input type="Text" name="firstname" value="<?php echo
$myrow["firstname"]; ?>">
</td></tr>
        <tr>
           <td align=left>Last Name :</td>
           <td align=left>
```

```
<input type="Text" name="lastname" value="<?php echo
$myrow["lastname"]; ?>">
</td></tr>
-->
        <tr>
          <td align=left>Email Address :</td>
          <td align=left><?php echo $myrow["email"];
?></td></tr>
<tr>
    <td align=left>New Email Address? :</td>
    <td align=left><input type="Text" name="newemail"
value="">
</td></tr>
<!--
<tr><td align=left>
Last Login:</td>
<td align=left> <?php print $myrow["last_login"];
?></td></tr>
<tr><td align=left>Account created:</td>
<td align=left> <?php echo $myrow["registered"];
?></td></tr>
-->
<tr><td>
<br>
<input type="Submit" name="submit" value="Update
information">
<br/><br/>
<input type="Submit" name="deleteuser" value="Delete User">
</td></tr>

<?php
$referer = isset($_SERVER['HTTP_REFERER']) ?
$_SERVER['HTTP_REFERER'] : '' ; // assign '' or any default
value;
   if (!$referer == '') {
      echo '<tr><td><br/><a href="' . $referer . '"
title="Return to the previous page">&laquo; Go
back</a></td></tr>';
   } else {
```

```php
        echo '<tr><td><br/><a href="javascript:history.go(-
1)" title="Return to the previous page">&laquo; Go
back</a></td></tr>';
    }
?>
<tr><td><br/>
<a href="<?php echo
$_SERVER['PHP_SELF']."?viewall=viewall"; ?>">View list</a>
</td></tr>

<tr><td>
<a href="<?php  echo $_SERVER['PHP_SELF']; ?>">Main
Menu</a>
</td></tr>
    </form>
</table>

<?php
}
}

// show a list of all users

} elseif($viewall){

 // display list of users
$result_all = mysqli_query($con, "SELECT id,username FROM
user order by username LIMIT $offset, $limit");

print("There are currently <b>$total</b> Users.");
print("<br/><br/>\n");

while ($myrow = mysqli_fetch_array($result_all)) {
printf("<a href=\"%s?uid=%s\">%s</a><br/>\n",
$_SERVER['PHP_SELF'],
$myrow["id"], $myrow["username"]);
}

print "<br/>". get_nav($offset, $limit, $total);
```

```php
?>
</td></tr>

<tr><td><br/>
<a href="<?php echo
$_SERVER['PHP_SELF']."?viewall=viewall"; ?>">View list</a>
</td></tr>

<tr><td>
<a href="<?php echo $_SERVER['PHP_SELF']; ?>">Main Menu</a>

<?php

// main page of user admin application

} else{

print "";
print("There are currently <b>$total</b> Users.");
print("<br/><br/>\n");
print "Search by letter<p>";

for ($i = 65 ; $i < 91 ; $i++){

// if $i is non-zero and is divisible by 5 print a line
break.
//# Create a new row every five columns
if (($i % 5 == 0) && ($i!=0)){
 echo "<br />";
}
//# Add a column
printf ('<a href = "%s?let=%s">%s</a> ',
$_SERVER['PHP_SELF'], chr($i+32), chr($i));
}

?>
<br/><br/>
```

```
<form method="post" action="<?php echo
$_SERVER['SCRIPT_NAME']; ?>">
Search for: <input type="text" name="searchwords"
value=""><br>
<input type="submit" name="finduser" value="Find User">
</form>

<br/><br/> Or View all Users
<form method="post" action="<?php echo
$_SERVER['SCRIPT_NAME']; ?>">
<input type=submit name="viewall" value="Viewall">
</form>

<?php
}
?>
</td></tr>
</table>

<?php

echo "<p><a href=\"logout.php\">Logout</a></p>";
}

function get_nav($offset, $limit, $totalnum, $type =
"normal") {
$navigation ='';

    if ($totalnum > $limit) {

//sprintf() returns the result as a formatted string vs
//printf() outputs the result as a formatted string
//if you use printf instead of sprintf in the function you
will notice a number
//being output along with everything else, this is because
printf returns
//the length of the outputted string.

  $navigation  .= sprintf('<table><tr><td>');
```

```php
    // Print File # - # of # (Customize to your need here)
  $navigation   .= sprintf('Record(s) %s', ( $offset + 1 ));
      $navigation   .= sprintf(' - ');
    if( $offset + $limit >= $totalnum ){
      $navigation   .= sprintf($totalnum);
    }else{ $navigation   .= sprintf ( $offset + $limit ); }
$navigation   .= sprintf(' of %s     |    </td>', $totalnum);

$navigation   .= sprintf('<td>Page </td>',"\n");

//print previous
if ($offset != 0) {
    $boffset = $offset-$limit;
if($type=='letter'){
$navigation .= sprintf('<td><a
href="%s?let=%s&offset=%s"><<<</a></td>',
        $_SERVER['PHP_SELF'],$GLOBALS['let'],$boffset);
}elseif($type =='usersearch'){
$navigation .= sprintf('<td><a
href="%s?finduser=yes&offset=%s&searchwords=%s"><<<</a></td>
',

$_SERVER['PHP_SELF'],$boffset,urlencode($GLOBALS['searchwor
ds']));
}
else{
$navigation .= sprintf('<td><a
href="%s?viewall=viewall&offset=%s"><<<</a></td>',
$_SERVER['PHP_SELF'],$boffset);
}
}

// calculate number of pages needing links
$pages = intval($totalnum/$limit);

// $pages now contains int of pages needed unless there is
a remainder from division
if ($totalnum%$limit) $pages++;
```

```php
//print pages
for ($i=1; $i <= $pages; $i++) { // loop thru
$newoffset=$limit*($i-1);
if ($newoffset != $offset) {
if($type=='letter'){
$navigation .= sprintf('<td><a
href="%s?let=%s&offset=%s">%s</a></td>%s',
        $_SERVER['PHP_SELF'], $GLOBALS['let'], $newoffset,
$i, "\n");
}
elseif($type =='usersearch'){
$navigation .= sprintf('<td><a
href="%s?finduser=yes&offset=%s&searchwords=%s">%s</a></td>
%s',
    $_SERVER['PHP_SELF'],
$newoffset,urlencode($GLOBALS['searchwords']), $i, "\n");
}
else{
$navigation .= sprintf('<td><a
href="%s?viewall=viewall&offset=%s">%s</a></td>%s',
$_SERVER['PHP_SELF'], $newoffset, $i, "\n");
}
}
else {
$navigation .= sprintf('<td>%s</td>%s', $i, "\n");
}
}

//print next
$noffset = $pages*$limit-$limit;
if ($offset != $noffset){
    $boffset = $offset+$limit;
if($type=='letter'){
$navigation .= sprintf('<td><a
href="%s?let=%s&offset=%s">>></a></td>',
        $_SERVER['PHP_SELF'], $GLOBALS['let'], $boffset);
}
elseif($type =='usersearch'){
```

```php
$navigation .= sprintf('<td><a
href="%s?finduser=yes&offset=%s&searchwords=%s">>></a></td>
',
        $_SERVER['PHP_SELF'],
$boffset,urlencode($GLOBALS['searchwords']));
}
else{
$navigation .= sprintf('<td><a
href="%s?viewall=viewall&offset=%s">>></a></td>',
        $_SERVER['PHP_SELF'], $boffset);
}
}
$navigation .= sprintf('</tr></table>');
}

else {
$navigation = "";
}

return $navigation;
}

?>
```

MySQLi Object-Oriented

```php
<?php
session_start();

date_default_timezone_set("America/New_York");

error_reporting(E_ALL);
ini_set('display_errors', '1');

require( 'database.php' );

if (!isset($_SESSION['loggedin'])) {
    die("Not logged in"); //this causes to script to stop
executing and lets the user know there is a problem

/*
Note:  instead of the die() function, you could use the
echo() function and provide an HTML link back to the login
page, or use the header() function to just redirect users
to the login page without any message. It is up to you to
decide how your application should function.
*/
}

elseif (isset($_SESSION['loggedin']) &&
($_SESSION['adminuser']=='0') ){  //logged in and NOT an
Admin
die("You do not have the right privileges to access this
page");
}

elseif (isset($_SESSION['loggedin']) &&
($_SESSION['adminuser']=='1') ){  //logged in and an Admin

/* what a user would be able to do if logged in and the
Admin. It is up to you to decide how your application
should function. */
```

```php
echo "Logged in as: {$_SESSION['loggedinuser']} -
[ADMIN]<br/><br/>\n";

?>

<table border="0" cellpadding="3" cellspacing="0"
width="500">
  <tr><td align="left" valign="top" width="500">

<?php
//setup variables

$let = '' ; // assign default value
$finduser = '' ; // assign default value
$uid = '' ; // assign default value
$viewall = '' ; // assign default value
$searchwords = '' ; // assign default value
$id = '' ; // assign default value
$username = '' ; // assign default value
$err = '' ; // assign default value
$clause = '' ; // assign default value

 // count users
$totalquery = $con->query("SELECT id FROM user");
$total = $totalquery->num_rows;

//sets the values for the variables regardless of GET/POST
method
if(isset($_POST['viewall'])){
    $viewall = $_POST['viewall'];
} else {
if(isset($_GET['viewall'])){
    $viewall = $_GET['viewall'];
}}

if(isset($_GET['let'])){
    //echo "<p>1 - {$_GET['let']}</p>";
```

```php
    //mysqli_real_escape_string requires two variables;
the connection variable, and the string variable.
    $let = $con->real_escape_string($_GET['let']);

    //echo "<p>2 - $let</p>";
}

if(isset($_POST['finduser'])){
    $finduser = $_POST['finduser'];
}else {
if(isset($_GET['finduser'])){
    $finduser = $_GET['finduser'];
}}

if(isset($_POST['searchwords'])){
    $searchwords = $con->real_escape_string(
$_POST['searchwords']);
}else {
if(isset($_GET['searchwords'])){
    $searchwords = $_GET['searchwords'];
}}

if(isset($_GET['uid'])){
    $uid = $con->real_escape_string($_GET['uid']);
} else {
if(isset($_POST['uid'])){
    $uid = $con->real_escape_string($_POST['uid']);
}}

//Set this to the number of records per page
$limit = 5;

if(isset($_GET['offset'])){
    $offset = $con->real_escape_string($_GET['offset']);
}
else{
//Set the initial offset
if (!isset($offset)) $offset = 0;
}
```

```php
// search for users by the first letter in username

if ($let){
$letter_total= $con->query("select id,username from user
where username like '$let%'");
$numrows_letter= $letter_total->num_rows;

$letter= $con->query("select id,username from user where
username like '$let%' LIMIT $offset, $limit");

function mysqli_result($result, $iRow = 0, $sField = '')
{
    $return = false;
    if ($result->data_seek($iRow))
    {
        $record = $result->fetch_array();
        if (empty($sField) && isset($record[0]))
        {
            $return = $record[0];
        }
        elseif (!empty($sField) && isset($record[$sField]))
        {
            $return = $record[$sField];
        }
    }
    return $return;
}


 if ($letter->num_rows > 0) {
     $row = $letter->fetch_array(MYSQLI_NUM);

        $numrows= $letter->num_rows;

        $x=0;
        while ($x<$numrows){

 $id= mysqli_result($letter,$x, 'id');
```

```php
$username= mysqli_result($letter,$x, 'username');
 //$letter->data_seek($x);
 //while ($row = $letter->fetch_array(MYSQLI_ASSOC)){
 //printf("<a href=\"%s?uid=%s\">%s</a><br/>\n",
$_SERVER['PHP_SELF'],$row[id], $row[username]);
 //}
printf("<a href=\"%s?uid=%s\">%s</a><br/>\n",
$_SERVER['PHP_SELF'],$id, $username);
        $x++;


        }
//print "<br/>". get_nav_letter($offset, $limit,
$numrows_letter);
print "<br/>". get_nav($offset, $limit,
$numrows_letter,"letter");

?>
</td></tr>
<tr><td>
<a href="<?php echo
$_SERVER['PHP_SELF']."?viewall=viewall"; ?>">View list</a>
</td></tr>
<tr><td>
<a href="<?php echo $_SERVER['PHP_SELF']; ?>">Main Menu</a>
<?php
 }
else{
print "<tr><td align=left colSpan=3 valign=top width=500>
    No records found for letter <b>$let</b></td></tr>";
?>
<tr><td><br/>
<a href="<?php echo
$_SERVER['PHP_SELF']."?viewall=viewall"; ?>">View list</a>
</td></tr>
<tr><td>
<a href="<?php echo $_SERVER['PHP_SELF']; ?>">Main Menu</a>
<?php

   }
```

```php
// if passed searchwords

} elseif ($finduser){

//if (!ereg("[[:alnum:]]",$searchwords)):
if (!preg_match('/[[:alnum:]]/i', $searchwords)){
echo "<p>Your <font color=\"#FF0000\"><b>search</b></font>
must be alphanumeric characters.";
echo "<br/>Letters a-z and numbers 0-9.</p>";

} else {

//add or remove fields to search to array
$fieldstosearch = array("username","email");

for($i=0;$i<count($fieldstosearch);$i++) {
$clause .= sprintf("(%s LIKE '%%%s%%') OR ",
$fieldstosearch[$i], urldecode($searchwords));
}
//use substring function to remove last four characters
from clause
if(count($fieldstosearch) > 1) {
$clause = "(".substr($clause, 0, -4).")";
}
else {
$clause = substr($clause, 0, -4);

}
//print field(s) query, this is optional
print $clause."<p>";

$searchq = $con->query("SELECT id from user WHERE
$clause");
$numrows_search =$searchq->num_rows;

$realsql = "SELECT * from user WHERE $clause LIMIT $offset,
$limit";
$result = $con->query($realsql);
```

```php
if ($result->num_rows > 0) {
$itemnum=$offset+1;
while($row = $result->fetch_array()) {
printf("%s <a href=\"%s?uid=%s\">%s</a><br/>\n",
$itemnum++, $_SERVER['PHP_SELF'],
$row["id"], $row["username"]);
}
}
else {
print "Sorry No records found";
}

print "<br/>". get_nav($offset, $limit, $numrows_search,
"usersearch");

}
?>

<tr><td><br/>
<a href="<?php echo
$_SERVER['PHP_SELF']."?viewall=viewall"; ?>">View list</a>
</td></tr>
<tr><td>
<a href="<?php echo $_SERVER['PHP_SELF']; ?>">Main Menu</a>

<?php
// if passed the userid take one of several actions after
pulling up user profile

} elseif ($uid){

// if the delete button is pressed, delete user
if(isset($_POST['deleteuser'])){

$delete = $con->query("delete from user WHERE id=$uid");
?>
<tr><td align=left colspan=3 valign=top width=500><b>
<?php print("User has been deleted"); ?>
</b></td></tr>
```

```php
<tr><td><br/>
<a href="<?php echo
$_SERVER['PHP_SELF']."?viewall=viewall"; ?>">View list</a>
</td></tr>
<tr><td>
<a href="<?php echo $_SERVER['PHP_SELF']; ?>">Main Menu</a>
<?php
}

// if new information is submitted, update the user
information
else{
if (isset($_POST['submit'])) {

if($_POST['newpassword'] !=''){

//if (!ereg("^[A-Za-z0-9]{4,12}$",$_POST['newpassword'])){
if (!preg_match("/^[A-Za-z0-
9]{4,12}$/i",$_POST['newpassword'])){
$err ="<tr>
<td align=left colspan=3 valign=top width=356><b>
Your <font color=\"#9c2108\">Password</font>:
<br/>-must be 4-12 characters long<br/>-can contain numbers
<br/>-cannot contain spaces<br/>-cannot contain non-
alphanumeric symbols such as \".?!#@$%*&\"
</b></td></tr>\n";
}
else{
$_POST['newpassword'] = md5($_POST['newpassword']);
//encrypt password
$sql = "UPDATE user SET password='".
$con->real_escape_string($_POST['newpassword'])."'
WHERE id='$uid'";
$result = $con->query($sql);
}
}

/*
```

```php
//if your user table stored firstname and lastname, you
would also update them if necessary
$sql3 = "UPDATE user SET lastname="'.$_POST['lastname']. "'
WHERE id=$uid";
$sql2 = "UPDATE user SET firstname='".$_POST['firstname'].
"' WHERE id=$uid";
*/

if($_POST['newemail'] !=''){
//use preg_match
//if(!preg_match('/^[[:alnum:]][a-z0-9_.-]*@[a-z0-9.-
]+\.[a-z]{2,4}$/i', $_POST['newemail'])){

  //FILTER_VALIDATE_EMAIL filter validates value as an e-
mail address.
if(!filter_var($_POST['newemail'], FILTER_VALIDATE_EMAIL)){
 $err .= "<tr>
 <td align=left colspan=3 valign=top width=500><b>
 Your <font color=\"#9c2108\">E-mail address </font>
 is not valid. </b></td></tr>\n";}
else{
$sql1= "UPDATE user SET email='".
$con->real_escape_string($_POST['newemail'])."'
WHERE id='$uid'";
$result1 = $con->query($sql1);
}
}

/*
//if your user table stored firstname and lastname, you
would also update them if necessary
$result3 = $con->query($sql3);
$result2 = $con->query($sql2);
*/


if(!$err){

?>
```

```php
  <tr><td align=left colspan=3 valign=top width=500><b>Thank
you! Information updated:</b>
<br/><br/>

<a href="<?php echo $_SERVER['PHP_SELF']."?uid=$uid";
?>">View updated record</a></td></tr>
<?php
}
else{
print ("$err");
print ("<tr><td align=left colspan=3 valign=top width=500>
<a href=\"".$_SERVER['PHP_SELF']."?uid=$uid\">
Go Back.</a></td></tr>");

}
?>

<tr><td><br/>
<a href="<?php echo
$_SERVER['PHP_SELF']."?viewall=viewall"; ?>">View list</a>
</td></tr>
<tr><td>
<a href="<?php echo $_SERVER['PHP_SELF']; ?>">Main Menu</a>
<?php

   } else {

// display the user profile

    // query the DB

    $sql = "SELECT * FROM user WHERE id='$uid'";

    //echo "$sql<br/>";
    $result = $con->query($sql);
    $myrow = $result->fetch_array();

   // echo $con->error();
    ?>
```

```
<p>
<b>
<font color="#9c2108">member: <?php echo
$myrow["username"]; ?></font>
</b>
</p>

<br/>

<form method="post" action="<?php echo
$_SERVER['SCRIPT_NAME']; ?>">
<input type=hidden name="uid" value="<?php echo
$myrow["id"]; ?>">

<table border="0" cellpadding="1" cellspacing="0">
        <tr>
           <td align=left width=150>Username :</td>
           <td align=left width=350>
           <?php echo $myrow["username"] ?> </td></tr>
        <tr>
           <td align=left>Present Password :</td>
 <td align=left>
 <?php echo $myrow["password"] ?></td></tr>
<tr>
           <td align=left>New password? :</td>
           <td align=left><input type="password"
name="newpassword" value="">
</td></tr>
<!-- if your user table stored firstname and lastname, you
would output the stored values in fields for update
<tr>
           <td align=left>First Name :</td>
           <td align=left>
<input type="Text" name="firstname" value="<?php echo
$myrow["firstname"]; ?>">
</td></tr>
        <tr>
           <td align=left>Last Name :</td>
```

```
            <td align=left>
<input type="Text" name="lastname" value="<?php echo
$myrow["lastname"]; ?>">
</td></tr>
-->

        <tr>
          <td align=left>Email Address :</td>
          <td align=left><?php echo $myrow["email"];
?></td></tr>
<tr>
    <td align=left>New Email Address? :</td>
    <td align=left><input type="Text" name="newemail"
value="">
</td></tr>
<!--
<tr><td align=left>
Last Login:</td>
<td align=left> <?php print $myrow["last_login"];
?></td></tr>
<tr><td align=left>Account created:</td>
<td align=left> <?php echo $myrow["registered"];
?></td></tr>
-->
<tr><td>
<br>
<input type="Submit" name="submit" value="Update
information">
<br/><br/>
<input type="Submit" name="deleteuser" value="Delete User">
</td></tr>

<?php
$referer = isset($_SERVER['HTTP_REFERER']) ?
$_SERVER['HTTP_REFERER'] : '' ; // assign '' or any default
value;
    if (!$referer == '') {
        echo '<tr><td><br/><a href="' . $referer . '"
title="Return to the previous page">&laquo; Go
back</a></td></tr>';
```

```php
    } else {
        echo '<tr><td><br/><a href="javascript:history.go(-
1)" title="Return to the previous page">&laquo; Go
back</a></td></tr>';
    }
?>
<tr><td><br/>
<a href="<?php echo
$_SERVER['PHP_SELF']."?viewall=viewall"; ?>">View list</a>
</td></tr>

<tr><td>
<a href="<?php  echo $_SERVER['PHP_SELF']; ?>">Main
Menu</a>
</td></tr>
    </form>
</table>

<?php
}
}

// show a list of all users

} elseif($viewall){

 // display list of users
$result_all = $con->query("SELECT id,username FROM user
order by username LIMIT $offset, $limit");

print("There are currently <b>$total</b> Users.");
print("<br/><br/>\n");

while ($myrow = $result_all->fetch_array()) {
printf("<a href=\"%s?uid=%s\">%s</a><br/>\n",
$_SERVER['PHP_SELF'],
$myrow["id"], $myrow["username"]);
}
```

```php
print "<br/>". get_nav($offset, $limit, $total);

?>
</td></tr>

<tr><td><br/>
<a href="<?php echo
$_SERVER['PHP_SELF']."?viewall=viewall"; ?>">View list</a>
</td></tr>

<tr><td>
<a href="<?php echo $_SERVER['PHP_SELF']; ?>">Main Menu</a>
<?php

// main page of user admin application

} else{

print "";
print("There are currently <b>$total</b> Users.");
print("<br/><br/>\n");
print "Search by letter<p>";

for ($i = 65 ; $i < 91 ; $i++){

// if $i is non-zero and is divisible by 5 print a line
break.
//# Create a new row every five columns
if (($i % 5 == 0) && ($i!=0)){
 echo "<br />";
}

//# Add a column
printf ('<a href = "%s?let=%s">%s</a> ',
$_SERVER['PHP_SELF'], chr($i+32), chr($i));
}

?>
<br/><br/>
```

```php
<form method="post" action="<?php echo
$_SERVER['SCRIPT_NAME']; ?>">
Search for: <input type="text" name="searchwords"
value=""><br>
<input type="submit" name="finduser" value="Find User">
</form>

<br/><br/> Or View all Users
<form method="post" action="<?php echo
$_SERVER['SCRIPT_NAME']; ?>">
<input type=submit name="viewall" value="Viewall">
</form>

<?php
}
?>
</td></tr>
</table>

<?php

echo "<p><a href=\"logout.php\">Logout</a></p>";
}

function get_nav($offset, $limit, $totalnum, $type =
"normal") {
$navigation ='';

    if ($totalnum > $limit) {

//sprintf() returns the result as a formatted string vs
//printf() outputs the result as a formatted string
//if you use printf instead of sprintf in the function you
will notice a number
//being output along with everything else, this is because
printf returns
//the length of the outputted string.

  $navigation  .= sprintf('<table><tr><td>');
```

```php
    // Print File # - # of # (Customize to your need here)
 $navigation  .= sprintf('Record(s) %s', ( $offset + 1 ));
      $navigation  .= sprintf(' - ');
    if( $offset + $limit >= $totalnum ){
      $navigation  .= sprintf($totalnum);
    }else{ $navigation  .= sprintf ( $offset + $limit ); }
$navigation  .= sprintf(' of %s    |    </td>', $totalnum);

$navigation  .= sprintf('<td>Page </td>',"\n");

//print previous
if ($offset != 0) {
    $boffset = $offset-$limit;
if($type=='letter'){
$navigation .= sprintf('<td><a
href="%s?let=%s&offset=%s"><<</a></td>',
        $_SERVER['PHP_SELF'],$GLOBALS['let'],$boffset);
}elseif($type =='usersearch'){
$navigation .= sprintf('<td><a
href="%s?finduser=yes&offset=%s&searchwords=%s"><<</a></td>
',

$_SERVER['PHP_SELF'],$boffset,urlencode($GLOBALS['searchwor
ds']));
}
else{
$navigation .= sprintf('<td><a
href="%s?viewall=viewall&offset=%s"><<</a></td>',
$_SERVER['PHP_SELF'],$boffset);
}
}

// calculate number of pages needing links
$pages = intval($totalnum/$limit);

// $pages now contains int of pages needed unless there is
a remainder from division
if ($totalnum%$limit) $pages++;
```

```
//print pages
for ($i=1; $i <= $pages; $i++) { // loop thru
$newoffset=$limit*($i-1);
if ($newoffset != $offset) {
if($type=='letter'){
$navigation .= sprintf('<td><a
href="%s?let=%s&offset=%s">%s</a></td>%s',
        $_SERVER['PHP_SELF'], $GLOBALS['let'], $newoffset,
$i, "\n");
}
elseif($type =='usersearch'){
$navigation .= sprintf('<td><a
href="%s?finduser=yes&offset=%s&searchwords=%s">%s</a></td>
%s',
    $_SERVER['PHP_SELF'],
$newoffset,urlencode($GLOBALS['searchwords']), $i, "\n");
}
else{
$navigation .= sprintf('<td><a
href="%s?viewall=viewall&offset=%s">%s</a></td>%s',
$_SERVER['PHP_SELF'], $newoffset, $i, "\n");
}
}
else {
$navigation .= sprintf('<td>%s</td>%s', $i, "\n");
}
}

//print next
$noffset = $pages*$limit-$limit;
if ($offset != $noffset){
    $boffset = $offset+$limit;
if($type=='letter'){
$navigation .= sprintf('<td><a
href="%s?let=%s&offset=%s">>></a></td>',
        $_SERVER['PHP_SELF'], $GLOBALS['let'], $boffset);
}
elseif($type =='usersearch'){
```

```php
$navigation .= sprintf('<td><a
href="%s?finduser=yes&offset=%s&searchwords=%s">>></a></td>
',
        $_SERVER['PHP_SELF'],
$boffset,urlencode($GLOBALS['searchwords']));
}
else{
$navigation .= sprintf('<td><a
href="%s?viewall=viewall&offset=%s">>></a></td>',
        $_SERVER['PHP_SELF'], $boffset);
}
}
$navigation .= sprintf('</tr></table>');
}

else {
$navigation = "";
}

return $navigation;
}

?>
```

PHP Data Object

```php
<?php
session_start();

date_default_timezone_set("America/New_York");

error_reporting(E_ALL);
ini_set('display_errors', '1');

require( 'database.php' );

if (!isset($_SESSION['loggedin'])) {
   die("Not logged in"); //this causes the script to stop
executing and lets the user know there is a problem

/*
Note:  instead of the die() function, you could use the
echo() function and provide an HTML link back to the login
page, or use the header() function to just redirect users
to the login page without any message. It is up to you to
decide what your application should function.
*/
}

elseif (isset($_SESSION['loggedin']) &&
($_SESSION['adminuser']=='0') ){  //logged in and NOT an
Admin
die("You do not have the right privileges to access this
page");
}

elseif (isset($_SESSION['loggedin']) &&
($_SESSION['adminuser']=='1') ){  //logged in and an Admin
```

```php
/* what a user would be able to do if logged in and the
Admin. It is up to you to decide how your application
should function. */
echo "Logged in as: {$_SESSION['loggedinuser']} -
[ADMIN]<br/><br/>\n";

?>

<table border="0" cellpadding="3" cellspacing="0"
width="500">
  <tr><td align="left" valign="top" width="500">

<?php
//setup variables

$let = '' ; // assign default value
$finduser = '' ; // assign default value
$uid = '' ; // assign default value
$viewall = '' ; // assign default value
$searchwords = '' ; // assign default value
$id = '' ; // assign default value
$username = '' ; // assign default value
$err = '' ; // assign default value
$clause = '' ; // assign default value

// count users
// If your SQL contains no variables, using a plain query
makes better sense than a prepared query

/*  $totalquery = $con->query("SELECT id FROM user");
  $rows = $totalquery->fetchAll(); //this may not be a good
idea with large data sets
  //print_r($rows);

$total = count($rows);
*/

  $totalquery = $con->query("SELECT count(id) FROM user");
  $rows = $totalquery->fetchColumn();
```

```
$total = $rows;

/*
Note do not use PDOStatement::rowCount to count the number
of rows returned by a SELECT statement.

' PDOStatement::rowCount() returns the number of rows
affected by the last DELETE, INSERT, or UPDATE statement
executed by the corresponding PDOStatement object.

If the last SQL statement executed by the associated
PDOStatement was a SELECT statement, some databases may
return the number of rows returned by that statement.
However, this behaviour is not guaranteed for all databases
and should not be relied on for portable applications. '
*/

//sets the values for the variables regardless of GET/POST
method
if(isset($_POST['viewall'])){
    $viewall = $_POST['viewall'];
} else {
if(isset($_GET['viewall'])){
    $viewall = $_GET['viewall'];
}}

if(isset($_GET['let'])){
    //echo "<p>1 - {$_GET['let']}</p>";
    //mysqli_real_escape_string requires two variables; the
connection variable, and the string variable.
    $let = $_GET['let'];
    //echo "<p>2 - $let</p>";
}

if(isset($_POST['finduser'])){
    $finduser = $_POST['finduser'];
}else {
if(isset($_GET['finduser'])){
```

```php
    $finduser = $_GET['finduser'];
}}

if(isset($_POST['searchwords'])){
    $searchwords = $_POST['searchwords'];
}else {
if(isset($_GET['searchwords'])){
    $searchwords = $_GET['searchwords'];
}}

if(isset($_GET['uid'])){
    $uid= $_GET['uid'];
} else {
if(isset($_POST['uid'])){
    $uid = $_POST['uid'];
}}

//Set this to the number of records per page
$limit = 5;

if(isset($_GET['offset'])){
    $offset= $_GET['offset'];
}
else{
//Set the initial offset
if (!isset($offset)) $offset = 0;
}

// search for users by the first letter in username

if ($let){

try{
$letter_total= $con->prepare("select count(*) from (select
distinct id,username from user where username like
CONCAT(?, '%')) u");

$letter_total->bindParam('1', $let, PDO::PARAM_STR);
$letter_total->execute();
```

```
}
 catch (PDOException $e)
{
     $error = 'Error: ' . $e->getMessage();
     echo $error;
     //exit();
}

$numrows_letter = $letter_total->fetchColumn();
//echo $numrows_letter;

// Close the cursor
/* The following call to closeCursor() may be required by
some drivers */
$letter_total->closeCursor();

try{
$letter= $con->prepare("select id,username from user where
username like CONCAT(?, '%') LIMIT ?, ?");
//echo $con->error;
//$letter->bindParam('sdd', $let, $offset, $limit);
$letter->bindParam(1, $let, PDO::PARAM_STR);
$letter->bindParam(2, $offset, PDO::PARAM_INT);
$letter->bindParam(3, $limit, PDO::PARAM_INT);
$letter->execute();

    // Bind by column number
    $letter->bindColumn(1, $id);
    $letter->bindColumn(2, $username);

    /*
    // Bind by column name
    $letter->bindColumn('id', $id);
    $letter->bindColumn('username', $username);

    // You can also specify a data type when binding
columns
    $letter->bindColumn('id', $id, PDO::PARAM_INT);
```

```php
      $letter->bindColumn('username', $username,
PDO::PARAM_STR);
      */
}
 catch (PDOException $e)
{
      $error = 'Error: ' . $e->getMessage();
      echo $error;
      //exit();
}

 if ($numrows_letter > 0) {

 while ($letter->fetch()){

printf("<a href=\"%s?uid=%s\">%s</a><br/>\n",
$_SERVER['PHP_SELF'],$id, $username);

  }

// Close the cursor
/* The following call to closeCursor() may be required by
some drivers */
$letter->closeCursor();

print "<br/>". get_nav($offset, $limit,
$numrows_letter,"letter");

?>
</td></tr>
<tr><td>
<a href="<?php echo
$_SERVER['PHP_SELF']."?viewall=viewall"; ?>">View list</a>
</td></tr>
<tr><td>
<a href="<?php echo $_SERVER['PHP_SELF']; ?>">Main Menu</a>
<?php
  }
else{
```

```php
print "<tr><td align=left colSpan=3 valign=top width=500>
    No records found for letter <b>$let</b></td></tr>";
?>
<tr><td><br/>
<a href="<?php echo
$_SERVER['PHP_SELF']."?viewall=viewall"; ?>">View list</a>
</td></tr>
<tr><td>
<a href="<?php echo $_SERVER['PHP_SELF']; ?>">Main Menu</a>
<?php

    }

// if passed searchwords, try to find matching user(s)

} elseif ($finduser){

if (!preg_match('/[[:alnum:]]/i', $searchwords)){
echo "<p>Your <font color=\"#FF0000\"><b>search</b></font>
must be alphanumeric characters.";
echo "<br/>Letters a-z and numbers 0-9.</p>";

} else {

//add or remove fields to search to array
$fieldstosearch = array("username","email");

for($i=0;$i<count($fieldstosearch);$i++) {
$clause .= sprintf("(%s LIKE '%%%s%%') OR ",
$fieldstosearch[$i], urldecode($searchwords));
}

    //use substring function to remove last four characters
from clause
    if(count($fieldstosearch) > 1) {
        $clause = "(".substr($clause, 0, -4).")";
        }
        else {
        $clause = substr($clause, 0, -4);
```

```php
    }

    //print field(s) in query, this is optional
    print $clause."<p>";

    try{
    $searchq = $con->prepare("SELECT count(id) from
user WHERE $clause");
    $searchq->execute();

    }
     catch (PDOException $e)
    {
        $error = 'Error: ' . $e->getMessage();
        echo $error;
         //exit();
    }

    $numrows_search = $searchq->fetchColumn();

    try{
    $result = $con->prepare("SELECT id, username from
er WHERE $clause LIMIT $offset, $limit");
        $result->bindParam(1, $offset, PDO::PARAM_INT);
        $result->bindParam(2, $limit, PDO::PARAM_INT);
        $result->execute();

    // Bind by column number
    $result->bindColumn(1, $id);
    $result->bindColumn(2, $username);
     }
      catch (PDOException $e)
    {
        $error = 'Error: ' . $e->getMessage();
        echo $error;
         //exit();

    if ($numrows_search > 0) {
```

```
                    $itemnum=$offset+1;

                    while($row = $result->fetch()) {
                    printf("%s <a
href=\"%s?uid=%s\">%s</a><br/>\n", $itemnum++,
$_SERVER['PHP_SELF'], $id, $username);
                    }

        }
        else {
        print "Sorry No records found";
        }

print "<br/>". get_nav($offset, $limit, $numrows_search,
"usersearch");
}
?>

<tr><td><br/>
<a href="<?php echo
$_SERVER['PHP_SELF']."?viewall=viewall"; ?>">View list</a>
</td></tr>
<tr><td>
<a href="<?php echo $_SERVER['PHP_SELF']; ?>">Main Menu</a>

<?php
// if passed the userid, take one of several actions, after
pulling up the user profile
} elseif ($uid){

// if the delete button is pressed, delete user
if(isset($_POST['deleteuser'])){

try{
$delete = $con->prepare("delete from user WHERE id = ?");
$delete->bindParam(1, $uid, PDO::PARAM_INT);
$delete->execute();
}
 catch (PDOException $e)
```

```php
{
    $error = 'Error: ' . $e->getMessage();
    echo $error;
    //exit();
}

?>
<tr><td align=left colspan=3 valign=top width=500><b>
<?php print("User has been deleted"); ?>
</b></td></tr>

<tr><td><br/>
<a href="<?php echo
$_SERVER['PHP_SELF']."?viewall=viewall"; ?>">View list</a>
</td></tr>
<tr><td>
<a href="<?php echo $_SERVER['PHP_SELF']; ?>">Main Menu</a>
<?php
}

// if new information is submitted, update the user
information
else{
if (isset($_POST['submit'])) {

if($_POST['newpassword'] !=''){

if (!preg_match("/^[A-Za-z0-
9]{4,12}$/i",$_POST['newpassword'])){
$err ="<tr>
<td align=left colspan=3 valign=top width=356><b>
Your <font color=\"#9c2108\">Password</font>:
<br/>-must be 4-12 characters long<br/>-can contain numbers
<br/>-cannot contain spaces<br/>-cannot contain non-
alphanumeric symbols such as \".?!#@$%*&\"
</b></td></tr>\n";
}
else{
```

```php
$_POST['newpassword'] = md5($_POST['newpassword']);
//encrypt password

try{
$sql = "UPDATE user SET password = ? WHERE id = ?";
$changerecord1 = $con->prepare($sql);
$changerecord1->bindParam(1, $_POST['newpassword'],
PDO::PARAM_STR);
$changerecord1->bindParam(2, $uid, PDO::PARAM_INT);
$changerecord1->execute();
}
 catch (PDOException $e)
{
    $error = 'Error: ' . $e->getMessage();
    echo $error;
    //exit();
}


}
}

if($_POST['newemail'] !=''){
    //use preg_match
//if(!preg_match('/^[[:alnum:]][a-z0-9_.-]*@[a-z0-9.-
]+\.[a-z]{2,4}$/i', $_POST['newemail'])){

  //FILTER_VALIDATE_EMAIL filter validates value as an e-
mail address.
if(!filter_var($_POST['newemail'], FILTER_VALIDATE_EMAIL)){
 $err .= "<tr>
 <td align=left colspan=3 valign=top width=500><b>
 Your <font color=\"#9c2108\">E-mail address </font>
 is not valid. </b></td></tr>\n";}
else{

try{
$sql1= "UPDATE user SET email = ? WHERE id = ?";
$changerecord2= $con->prepare($sql1);
```

```php
$changerecord2->bindParam(1, $_POST['newemail'],
PDO::PARAM_STR);
$changerecord2->bindParam(2, $uid, PDO::PARAM_INT);
$changerecord2->execute();
}
 catch (PDOException $e)
{
     $error = 'Error: ' . $e->getMessage();
     echo $error;
     //exit();
}


}
}

/*
//if your user table stored firstname and lastname, you
would also update them if necessary
try{
$sql3 = "UPDATE user SET lastname = ? WHERE id = ?";
$changerecord3 = $con->prepare($sql3);
$changerecord3->bindParam(1, $_POST['lastname'],
PDO::PARAM_STR);
$changerecord3->bindParam(2, $uid, PDO::PARAM_INT);
$changerecord3->execute();
}
 catch (PDOException $e)
{
     $error = 'Error: ' . $e->getMessage();
     echo $error;
     //exit();
}

try{
$sql4 = "UPDATE user SET firstname = ? WHERE id = ?";
$changerecord4 = $con->prepare($sql4);
$changerecord4->bindParam(1, $_POST['firstname'],
PDO::PARAM_STR);
$changerecord4->bindParam(2, $uid, PDO::PARAM_INT);
```

```php
$changerecord4->execute();
}
 catch (PDOException $e)
{
    $error = 'Error: ' . $e->getMessage();
    echo $error;
    //exit();
}
*/


if(!$err){

?>
 <tr><td align=left colspan=3 valign=top width=500><b>Thank
you! Information updated:</b>
<br/><br/>

<a href="<?php echo $_SERVER['PHP_SELF']."?uid=$uid";
?>">View updated record</a></td></tr>
<?php
}
else{
print ("$err");
print ("<tr><td align=left colspan=3 valign=top width=500>
<a href=\"".$_SERVER['PHP_SELF']."?uid=$uid\">
Go Back.</a></td></tr>");

}
?>


<tr><td><br/>
<a href="<?php echo
$_SERVER['PHP_SELF']."?viewall=viewall"; ?>">View list</a>
</td></tr>
<tr><td>
<a href="<?php echo $_SERVER['PHP_SELF']; ?>">Main Menu</a>
<?php
```

```php
    } else {

// display the user profile

    // query the DB

    $sql = "SELECT * FROM user WHERE id = ?";

    try{
    $result = $con->prepare($sql);
    $result->bindParam(1, $uid, PDO::PARAM_INT);
     $result->execute();

     /* bind result variables */
    $result->bindColumn(1, $id);   //bind additional results
if needed
    $result->bindColumn(2, $username);
    $result->bindColumn(3, $password);
    $result->bindColumn(4, $email);
    $result->bindColumn(5, $level);
          }
     catch (PDOException $e)
    {
     $error = 'Error: ' . $e->getMessage();
         echo $error;
         //exit();
    }

         $result->fetch();
    ?>

<p>
<b>
<font color="#9c2108">member: <?php echo $username;
?></font>
</b>
</p>

<br/>
```

```html
<form method="post" action="<?php echo
$_SERVER['SCRIPT_NAME']; ?>">
<input type=hidden name="uid" value="<?php echo $id; ?>">

<table border="0" cellpadding="1" cellspacing="0">
        <tr>
            <td align=left width=150>Username :</td>
            <td align=left width=350>
            <?php echo $username; ?> </td></tr>
        <tr>
            <td align=left>Present Password :</td>
 <td align=left>
 <?php echo $password; ?></td></tr>
<tr>
            <td align=left>New password? :</td>
            <td align=left><input type="password"
name="newpassword" value="">
</td></tr>
<!-- if your user table stored firstname and lastname, you
would output the stored values in fields for update
<tr>
            <td align=left>First Name :</td>
            <td align=left>
<input type="Text" name="firstname" value="<?php echo
$firstname; ?>">
</td></tr>
        <tr>
            <td align=left>Last Name :</td>
            <td align=left>
<input type="Text" name="lastname" value="<?php echo
$lastname; ?>">
</td></tr>
-->
        <tr>
            <td align=left>Email Address :</td>
            <td align=left><?php echo $email; ?></td></tr>
<tr>
    <td align=left>New Email Address? :</td>
```

```
    <td align=left><input type="Text" name="newemail"
value="">
</td></tr>
<!--
<tr><td align=left>
Last Login:</td>
<td align=left> <?php print $last_login; ?></td></tr>
<tr><td align=left>Account created:</td>
<td align=left> <?php echo $registered; ?></td></tr>
-->
<tr><td>
<br>
<input type="Submit" name="submit" value="Update
information">
<br/><br/>
<input type="Submit" name="deleteuser" value="Delete User">
</td></tr>

<?php
$referer = isset($_SERVER['HTTP_REFERER']) ?
$_SERVER['HTTP_REFERER'] : '' ; // assign '' or any default
value
    if (!$referer == '') {
        echo '<tr><td><br/><a href="' . $referer . '"
title="Return to the previous page">&laquo; Go
back</a></td></tr>';
    } else {
        echo '<tr><td><br/><a href="javascript:history.go(-
1)" title="Return to the previous page">&laquo; Go
back</a></td></tr>';
    }
?>
<tr><td><br/>
<a href="<?php echo
$_SERVER['PHP_SELF']."?viewall=viewall"; ?>">View list</a>
</td></tr>

<tr><td>
```

```php
<a href="<?php  echo $_SERVER['PHP_SELF']; ?>">Main
Menu</a>
</td></tr>
    </form>
</table>

<?php
}
}

// show a list of all users

} elseif($viewall){
 // display list of users

// make sure the variables are set to the type PDO is
expecting when you bind the parameters
$offset = (int)$offset;
$limit = (int)$limit;

//echo '<br/>offset: '.$offset.'<br/>';
//echo '<br/>limit: '.$limit.'<br/>';

try{

/*** prepare the SQL statement ***/
$result_all = $con->prepare("SELECT id,username FROM user
order by username LIMIT ?, ?");

/*** bind the parameters ***/
$result_all->bindParam(1, $offset, PDO::PARAM_INT);
$result_all->bindParam(2, $limit, PDO::PARAM_INT);

/*** execute the prepared statement ***/
$result_all->execute();

/* Bind by column number */
$result_all->bindColumn(1, $id);
$result_all->bindColumn(2, $username);
```

```php
}
 catch (PDOException $e)
{
     $error = 'Error: ' . $e->getMessage();
     echo $error;
     //exit();
}

print("There are currently <b>$total</b> Users.");
print("<br/><br/>\n");

while ($result_all->fetch()) {
printf("<a href=\"%s?uid=%s\">%s</a><br/>\n",
$_SERVER['PHP_SELF'],
$id, $username);
}

print "<br/>". get_nav($offset, $limit, $total);

?>
</td></tr>

<tr><td><br/>
<a href="<?php echo
$_SERVER['PHP_SELF']."?viewall=viewall"; ?>">View list</a>
</td></tr>

<tr><td>
<a href="<?php echo $_SERVER['PHP_SELF']; ?>">Main Menu</a>
<?php

// main page of user admin application

} else {

print "";
print("There are currently <b>$total</b> Users.");
print("<br/><br/>\n");
print "Search by letter<p>";
```

```php
for ($i = 65 ; $i < 91 ; $i++){

// if $i is non-zero and is divisible by 5 print a line
break.
//# Create a new row every five columns
if (($i % 5 == 0) && ($i!=0)){
 echo "<br />";
}
//# Add a column
printf ('<a href = "%s?let=%s">%s</a> ',
$_SERVER['PHP_SELF'], chr($i+32), chr($i));
}

?>
<br/><br/>
<form method="post" action="<?php echo
$_SERVER['SCRIPT_NAME']; ?>">
Search for: <input type="text" name="searchwords"
value=""><br>
<input type="submit" name="finduser" value="Find User">
</form>

<br/><br/> Or View all Users
<form method="post" action="<?php echo
$_SERVER['SCRIPT_NAME']; ?>">
<input type=submit name="viewall" value="Viewall">
</form>

<?php
}
?>
</td></tr>
</table>

<?php

echo "<p><a href=\"logout.php\">Logout</a></p>";
}
```

```php
function get_nav($offset, $limit, $totalnum, $type =
"normal") {
$navigation ='';
    if ($totalnum > $limit) {

//sprintf() returns the result as a formatted string vs
//printf() outputs the result as a formatted string
//if you use printf instead of sprintf in the function you
will notice a number
//being output along with everything else, this is because
printf returns
//the length of the outputted string.

 $navigation .= sprintf('<table><tr><td>');
    // Print File # - # of # (Customize to your need here)
 $navigation .= sprintf('Record(s) %s', ( $offset + 1 ));
      $navigation .= sprintf(' - ');
    if( $offset + $limit >= $totalnum ){
      $navigation .= sprintf($totalnum);
    }else{ $navigation  .= sprintf ( $offset + $limit ); }
$navigation .= sprintf(' of %s     |   </td>', $totalnum);

$navigation .= sprintf('<td>Page </td>',"\n");

//print previous
if ($offset != 0) {
    $boffset = $offset-$limit;
if($type=='letter'){
$navigation .= sprintf('<td><a
href="%s?let=%s&offset=%s"><<</a></td>',
        $_SERVER['PHP_SELF'],$GLOBALS['let'],$boffset);
}elseif($type =='usersearch'){
$navigation .= sprintf('<td><a
href="%s?finduser=yes&offset=%s&searchwords=%s"><<</a></td>
',

$_SERVER['PHP_SELF'],$boffset,urlencode($GLOBALS['searchwor
ds']));
```

```
}
else{
$navigation .= sprintf('<td><a
href="%s?viewall=viewall&offset=%s"><<</a></td>',
$_SERVER['PHP_SELF'],$boffset);
}
}

// calculate number of pages needing links
$pages = intval($totalnum/$limit);

// $pages now contains int of pages needed unless there is
a remainder from division
if ($totalnum%$limit) $pages++;

//print pages
for ($i=1; $i <= $pages; $i++) { // loop thru
$newoffset=$limit*($i-1);
if ($newoffset != $offset) {
if($type=='letter'){
$navigation .= sprintf('<td><a
href="%s?let=%s&offset=%s">%s</a></td>%s',
        $_SERVER['PHP_SELF'], $GLOBALS['let'], $newoffset,
$i, "\n");
}
elseif($type =='usersearch'){
$navigation .= sprintf('<td><a
href="%s?finduser=yes&offset=%s&searchwords=%s">%s</a></td>
%s',
    $_SERVER['PHP_SELF'],
$newoffset,urlencode($GLOBALS['searchwords']), $i, "\n");
}
else{
$navigation .= sprintf('<td><a
href="%s?viewall=viewall&offset=%s">%s</a></td>%s',
$_SERVER['PHP_SELF'], $newoffset, $i, "\n");
}
}
else {
```

```php
$navigation .= sprintf('<td>%s</td>%s', $i, "\n");
  }
}

//print next
$noffset = $pages*$limit-$limit;
if ($offset != $noffset){
    $boffset = $offset+$limit;
if($type=='letter'){
$navigation .= sprintf('<td><a
href="%s?let=%s&offset=%s">>></a></td>',
        $_SERVER['PHP_SELF'], $GLOBALS['let'], $boffset);
}
elseif($type =='usersearch'){
$navigation .= sprintf('<td><a
href="%s?finduser=yes&offset=%s&searchwords=%s">>></a></td>
',
        $_SERVER['PHP_SELF'],
$boffset,urlencode($GLOBALS['searchwords']));
}
else{
$navigation .= sprintf('<td><a
href="%s?viewall=viewall&offset=%s">>></a></td>',
        $_SERVER['PHP_SELF'], $boffset);
}
}
$navigation .= sprintf('</tr></table>');
}

else {
$navigation = "";
}

return $navigation;
}

?>
```

Also By Onaje Johnston

Creating a User Registration Membership System (PHP Basic Recipe)

MySQLi Quick Start (PHP Basic Recipe)

PHP Data Objects Quick Start (PHP Basic Recipe)

Visit http://phpbasicrecipe.com to sign up for email announcements and more information about the series.

www.ingramcontent.com/pod-product-compliance
Lightning Source LLC
Chambersburg PA
CBHW080406060326
40689CB00019B/4146